Where Nature Reigns

The Wilderness Areas of the Southern Appalachians

Jack Horan

DOWN HOME™

Down Home Press, Asheboro, N.C.

First Printing, June 1997
1 2 3 4 5 6 7 8 9

ISBN 1-878086-58-8

Library of Congress Catalog Card Number
97-067131

Printed in the United States of America

Cover design by Tim Rickard.
Photographs by Jack Horan unless otherwise credited.
Book design by Beth Glover.
Cover photo by Donna Bise.

An extension of the copyright page
may be found on page 248 of this book.

Down Home Press
P.O. Box 4126
Asheboro, N.C. 27204

The Mountains that are the most considerable are the Charokee, or Appelapean Mountains, they take their rise from the North-west part of South Carolina, and so continue in one Ridge to the Northward for several hundred Miles, being in most places five or six hundred Miles from the Sea; they are vastly high, and abound with Trees, various kinds of Plants, and stones of several different Natures. Beyond these Mountains you have a prospect only of large Woods, Savannas, dismal Swamps and Forrests, being as is supposed, the Habitation of Savage Indians, and wild Beasts of various kinds.

— Historian John Brickell, *The Natural History of North-Carolina*, 1737, Johnson Reprint Corp., New York and London, 1969.

Acknowledgments

I would like to give special thanks and recognition to the many people who helped make this book possible. *Where Nature Reigns* would not have come together without their expertise, guidance and assistance.

First, I would like to gratefully acknowledge the contributions of Peter Kirby, southeastern regional director of The Wilderness Society in Atlanta.

Others who provided critical reviews and offered helpful suggestions were Paul Kalisz of Kentucky Forest Watch; Ernie Dickerman of Swoope, Va.; Cecil Frost of the Plant Protection Program of the North Carolina Department of Agriculture; Greg Good of Morgantown, W.Va.; Ginny Guthrie of Lexington, Ky.; Hugh Irwin of the Southern Appalachian Forest Coalition in Asheville, N.C.; Mike Leonard of Bethania, N.C.; Jim Loesel of Roanoke, Va.; Bob Long of Athens, Tenn.; Dr. Michael Pelton of the University of Tennessee; Alan S. Weakley, regional ecologist for the Southeast Regional Office of The Nature Conservancy in Chapel Hill, N.C.; Ken Wills of the Alabama Environmental Council in Birmingham; and Dr. Robert Zahner, retired professor of forestry from Clemson University.

From the national forests were Mary E. Gaines of the Bankhead and Talladega National Forests in Alabama; Karen O. Braddy and Jim Herd of the Chattahoochee National Forest in Georgia; Jorge Hersel and Marie T. Walker of the Daniel Boone National Forest in

Kentucky; Terry Seyden and Julie Trzeciak of the Nantahala and Pisgah National Forests in North Carolina; Bill Craig and Robert Palazzo of the Sumter National Forest in South Carolina; Wilma Marine and Terry McDonald of the Cherokee National Forest in Tennessee; Frank Bergmann, Alan R. McPherson, Terry Smith and Thomas E. Wright Jr. of the Jefferson and George Washington National Forests in Virginia; and Kate Goodrich of the Monongahela National Forest in West Virginia.

From the National Park Service were Suzanne S. Barrett of Cumberland National Historical Park; Nancy Gray and Bob Miller of Great Smoky Mountains National Park; Deanne Adams, Bill Cook, Reed Engle and Karen A. Michaud of Shenandoah National Park; Ron Wilson of Big South Fork National River and Recreation Area; and Paul Winegar of the Atlanta regional office.

From the Fish and Wildlife Service were Brian Cole, Bob Currie and Nora Murdock of the Asheville, N.C., field office; Gail S. Baker, Canaan Valley National Wildlife Refuge; Chris Lucash of the Red Wolf Project in Great Smoky Mountains National Park and Vicki Boatwright of the Atlanta regional office.

I also would like to express appreciation to Dustin Peck of KPC Photography in Charlotte, N.C., who printed most of the photographs that appear in this book; to Liz and Leskie Pinson, who hiked into Linville Gorge Wilderness for the front cover photograph; to Vic Weals of Knoxville, Tenn., for providing the photo of the chestnut trees; to my editor, Dot Jackson of Six Mile, S.C., whose keen-eyed editing and extensive knowledge of the Southern Appalachians proved invaluable; and to my wife, Rita, who accompanied me on most of my hiking trips into the wildernesses and identified many of the flowers, shrubs and trees that appear in the text.

Preface

Nature reigns in the wilderness areas of the Southern Appalachians.

These wildest of the region's wild lands have been set aside by Congress as part of the National Wilderness Preservation System. The system permanently protects 104 million acres from Alaska to Florida.

The wilderness areas of the Southern Appalachians contain 6,000-foot mountains, 1,000-foot-deep gorges and 400-foot-high waterfalls. They harbor barred owls and black bears, brook trout and bird's foot violets, Indiana bats and Indian paintbrush, marbled salamanders and mountain laurel, painted trillium and pine snakes, red spruce and rosebay rhododendron, yellow warblers and yellow birches. They protect water quality and filter out pollutants, safeguard scenery and biological diversity and offer quiet sanctuary for those who seek solitude.

These 47 wilderness areas, plus seven other proposed wildernesses and wilderness study areas, lie within national forests and national parks in Alabama, Georgia, Kentucky, North Carolina, South Carolina, Tennessee, Virginia and West Virginia.

The Wilderness Act of 1964 declared that wilderness is "an area where the Earth and its community of life are untrammeled by man, where man himself is a visitor who does not remain." The act imposes the nation's strictest conservation standards for lands. With some exceptions, the designation permanently bans roads, wheeled vehicles, logging, mining, power lines and developed trails and campsites. Most wildernesses have erased traces of human imprints such as trail signs, blazes and foot bridges. Visitors may only enter and leave on foot or, where permitted, on horseback.

Wilderness designation bans mountain bikes, all-terrain vehicles and snowmobiles. But it allows traditional recreational activities such as hiking, backpacking, fishing, and if previously permitted by land managers, hunting.

Combined, the 54 wildernesses and proposed wildernesses cover 1,047,486 acres. That represents the greatest concentration of wilderness east of the Mississippi River.

This book profiles the 54 areas, describing their natural history, landmarks and wildlife. The profiles are intended to provide readers with an appreciation of these areas as well as enough information that, combined with a detailed map and a compass, will allow them to explore some of the most remote and primitive lands in Eastern America.

I've hiked in all 54 areas, most of them two or three times, from Cheaha Wilderness in Alabama to Dolly Sods Wilderness in West Virginia. Each has its own distinctive appeal and splendor. I carry these images from hundreds of miles of exploration:

• The mink that scampered along a creek side in Laurel Fork South Wilderness in West Virginia on a summer afternoon, poking its head in and out of rock crevices as it hunted for prey.

• The blizzard-like storm that smothered Little Wilson Creek Wilderness in late fall, enveloping Virginia's Mount Rogers in thick, swirling clouds of snow.

• The white-tailed deer that burst from her hiding spot in tall grass three feet from where I stopped to check my trail map in Cohutta Wilderness in Georgia.

• The sharp pangs of pain that shot through bare feet during an early spring fording of the chilly Sipsey River in Sipsey Wilderness in Alabama.

• The wintry fog that froze into rime ice, forming a thick white glaze on every twig and grass blade on Unaka Mountain Wilderness in Tennessee.

• The sight of wood anemone, nodding trillium and sweet white violets that carpeted the forest floor of Ellicott Rock Wilderness in South Carolina.

• The dramatic, awe-inspiring vista of sandstone arches and pinnacles of Clifty Wilderness in Kentucky.

• The panoramic view from a mile-high grassy bald in Middle Prong Wilderness in North Carolina. The landscape of the Pisgah National Forest looked on that October day much the same as it did three centuries ago when the original wilderness spread seemingly without end, across mountain after mountain of the Southern Appalachians.

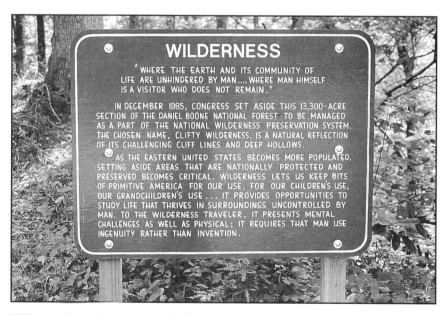

Wilderness sign marking boundary of Clifty Wilderness in Kentucky describes the philosophy underlying the National Wilderness Preservation System.

Contents

Virginia

West Virginia

Introduction

Let's go back three centuries. Let's take a 17th Century walk through the wilds of the Southeast to the "Appelapean" mountains, as they were known then.

We'll go with a group of imaginary explorers on a trek similar to those made by real-life explorers such as William Bartram, William Byrd and John Lederer. While a mythical journey, the sights and sounds are based on factual accounts.

It is spring. Our explorers land briefly on the coast, then pilot their ship through an inlet and up a tidal river. Formations of brown pelicans skim the water. Osprey and bald eagles dive for fish. In the distance whooping cranes glide over the marsh, their white and black feathers standing out sharply against the green cord grass.

The brackish water soon turns fresh. Thick-girthed bald cypress, Atlantic white cedar and tupelo now border the river. The water becomes shallow. The ship can go no farther. Our explorers anchor and get into their pinnace, a small ship's boat. Overhead, they glimpse flashes of orange, yellow and green. Flocks of squawking Carolina parakeets — 12-inch-long parrots — perch on the limbs of bald cypress trees.

At night, the swamp will resound with the hoots of barred owls, the howls of red wolves and the bellowing of alligators. Dawn brings the staccato tapping of the red-and-black ivory-billed woodpecker.

As the cypress forest closes in over the narrowing river, the explorers beach their pinnace and begin their overland journey.

Before them stands an unbroken parkland of longleaf pines. The tall, straight trees are charred from periodic wildfires. Orchids and pitcher plants compete with blazing stars and butterworts for a place in the savanna.

After 100 miles, sandy soil gives way to red clay. Pines and turkey oak yield to hickories, willow oaks and dogwoods. The flat land of the coastal plain changes into the rolling pitch of the Piedmont. White-tailed deer browse the forest edge, keeping out a wary eye for wolves. Raccoons prowl stream banks, digging out freshwater mussels that pave the gravelly stream bottoms.

As they follow a stream, our explorers halt in surprise. Ahead, several black bears wade in the water, their eyes fixed on wriggling fish. Throngs of river herring have come from the ocean to the shallow streams to lay their eggs. With swipes of their paws, the bears gaff enough fish to sate their post-winter hunger.

The sound of distant thunder rolls across the landscape. It's not an approaching storm but the drumming of beating wings. The wings are those of millions of passenger pigeons flying in a migratory flock. The flock is so large it takes an hour to pass.

Our explorers soon come upon a sea of green vegetation. It's a canebrake, a growth of native cane that reaches 30 feet high. The thick foliage muffles the deep-throated grunts and the clop of hoofed feet. A group of bison have retreated to the canebrake to escape the heat of the day.

Next, a Catawba Indian village comes into view. The Catawbas go on a hunt after dark. Carrying burning torches, they surround a huge oak festooned with resting passenger pigeons. The Catawbas use long poles to knock down hundreds of birds to replenish their larders.

The next morning, the forest opens into a treeless grassland. Our explorers wade through waist-high bluestem grass, sunflower and coneflower plants of this Piedmont prairie.

About 40 miles away, a purplish outline rises under puffy white clouds. The mountains lie ahead. The air chills; the streams gurgle louder; the fragrance of wildflowers mixes with a damp mossy smell. A panther, or mountain lion, lets out a long, wailing scream, beckoning to a mate or warning a rival.

The adventurers climb a bison trail through the foothills into the mountains. Purple rhododendron flowers overhang the streams, shadowing brook trout. Last fall's chestnuts lie scattered under mammoth chestnut trees. A black bear, nibbling on squaw root, bobs its head, then ambles off.

Upon a ridge, a shrill bleat pricks all ears. It's a female elk calling to her calf. Our explorers glance toward a wet meadow below. Dozens of elk, their heads bent, nip spring grasses amid stands of swamp pink. A bog lemming scuttles to the safety of cinnamon fern and golden club.

From the forest, a hunting party of Cherokee Indians silently moves into the bog. Arrows fly. An elk falls. The Cherokees move in, take the carcass and vanish into the trees.

At dusk, our explorers make camp on a high peak among red spruce and Fraser firs. Clouds drift in, dripping moisture. As the explorers build a fire, the mournful howl of gray wolves drifts up the ridge. The men grab their rifles. No need. The wolves are just gathering for their evening hunt. The howls eventually fade as the pack tracks the spoor of an elk or bison.

Weary but contented, our explorers lean back and gaze at the millions of sparkling pinpoints of stars in the black sky. They've reached their destination, the Appelapeans. The mysteries and magnificence of this vast wilderness await further exploration.

Panorama of mountains surrounds campers in North Carolina's Middle Prong Wilderness.

Great herds of Red and Fallow Deer I daily saw feeding; and on the hill-sides, Bears crashing Mast like Swine. Small Leopards I have seen in the Woods, but never any Lions, though their skins are much worn by Indians. The Wolves in these parts are so ravenous, that I often in the night feared my horse would be devoured by them, they would gather up and howl so close around about him, though Tether'd to the same tree at whose foot I myself and the Indian lay; but the Fires which we made, I suppose, scared them from worrying us all. Beaver and Otter I met with at every River that I passed; and the Woods are full of Grey Foxes.

— Explorer John Lederer, describing an area near the Virginia mountains in 1669. *The Discoveries of John Lederer*, University of Virginia Press, 1958.

Part 1

The Southern Appalachians

The original wilderness

A temperate climate, abundant moisture, deep soils and a long growing season make the Southern Appalachians a heaven on Earth for trees, flowering plants, mammals, birds, fish, amphibians and fungi.

The Southern Appalachians are part of the Appalachian mountain chain that stretches for nearly 2,000 miles from Canada to Alabama. The mountains arose about 300 million years ago, the result of upheavals caused by collisions between continental plates. Over the eons wind, rain, snow, ice and tiny organisms have chiseled and buffeted the peaks into their rounded and undulating profile.

The Southern Appalachians form the roof of Eastern America. The tallest peak, 6,684-foot-high Mount Mitchell in North Carolina, is the highest point east of the Rockies.

Anchoring the Southern Appalachian range at its northern extreme is Spruce Knob, at 4,861 feet the highest point in West Virginia. Cheaha Mountain, at 2,407 feet the tallest mountain in Alabama, stands as the southern sentinel.

The Southern Appalachians comprise eight physical provinces. On the eastern side, the Allegheny Mountains lie in northern Virginia and northern West Virginia. Moving south, the Northern Ridge and Valley section extends through central Virginia. Paralleling these ridges on the east is the range of the Blue Ridge, which continues on down through southern Virginia, western North Carolina and northern Georgia. At the southern extreme, the Southern Ridge and Valley section covers northwestern Georgia and central Alabama.

West of the Appalachian spine, the Northern Cumberland Mountains slice through southern West Virginia and western Virginia. The Central Ridge and Valley section spills across eastern Tennessee. The Northern Cumberland Plateau takes in eastern Kentucky; the Southern Cumberland Plateau embraces northern Alabama.

East and west, the mountains differ in both appearance and substance. The peak-and-valley Allegheny and Blue Ridge are made of hard igneous rock. The long, flatter Cumberland mountains are fashioned from softer sandstone and limestone.

Water works magic in the Southern Appalachians, which contains the wettest areas in the East. Moist winds from the Atlantic Ocean and the Gulf of Mexico continually sweep the mountains. Precipitation averages 60 to 80 inches a year. The higher elevations of West Virginia get from 120 to 150 inches of snow in a winter.

The region is one of the few places on Earth where tropical storms and blizzards alternately visit. The remnants of Hurricane Opal in 1995, Hurricane Hugo in 1989 and Hurricane Camille in 1969 raked parts of the mountains. The Superstorm of 1993 dumped from two to four feet of snow in Georgia, North Carolina, Tennessee and elsewhere. The Blizzard of 1996 dropped up to four feet of snow in northern Virginia and West Virginia.

This abundance of water sustains the mountains' misty mantle of green, the deciduous broad-leaved forest. Forester Maurice Brooks wrote that such woodlands can be found in Europe, in central China, and in a few other temperate-zone areas that lie 30 to 60 degrees of latitude from the Equator. "But the best and most extensive of these forests is in North America, on the slopes of and to either side of the Appalachians," Brooks concluded in his 1965 book, *The Appalachians*.

The deciduous trees combine with evergreen conifers to paint a kaleidoscope of color. The forest changes to rhythms set by the four seasons. Beneath the canopy, a boundless wild garden prospers. The northeast-southwest alignment of the Appalachians created a botanical refuge. During the last Ice Age 20,000 years ago, the favorable alignment allowed plants to migrate southward to escape advancing glaciers. The glaciers stopped short of the Southern Appalachians.

Here, north meets south. Northern plants live on cool mountain peaks at their southern limits; southern plants grow in warm, south-facing valleys at their northern limits.

As elevation rises, climate changes. Climbing 1,000 feet is equal to traveling 200 to 250 miles north. The climate on the highest peaks as far south as North Carolina and Tennessee mimics that of southern Canada. Elevation, the tilt of the land toward or away from the sun, greater or lesser amounts of rain and snow, all create a multitude of smaller niches within larger ones. The result is a stunning biological diversity.

The Southern Appalachians may contain more than 20,000 species of plants and animals, according to "The Southern Appalachian Assessment," a 1996 state of the science report. The region has 62 species of fish, 65 species of mammals, 80 species of amphibians and reptiles, 175 species of land birds, 2,250 species of vascular plants and perhaps as many as 25,000 invertebrates.

Great Smoky Mountains National Park in North Carolina and Tennessee alone has 100 species of native trees. That's more than all of northern Europe.

The dominant forest type is oak, followed by conifers such as pine, hemlock and spruce. Among the more common forest types are the oak-hickory forest of red oak, pignut hickory, red maple and black gum; the open oak-pine forest of white oak, scarlet oak, table mountain pine and white pine; and the northern hardwood forest of yellow birch, northern red oak and sugar maple. The cove hardwood forest consists of tulip-poplar, beech and magnolia; the spruce-fir forest consists of red spruce and Fraser fir. The mixed mesophytic forest, found mostly in Kentucky, Tennessee and West Virginia, is so named because no single tree dominates. The forest may have as many as 80 hardwood species.

At least 400 to 500 species of animals and plants are found nowhere else in the world, including 40 kinds of mosses and liverworts.

"All this adds up to the very high species richness of the Southern Appalachians," says Alan Weakley, Southeastern regional ecologist for The Nature Conservancy.

Four centuries ago, original wilderness cloaked the Southern Appalachians. The landscape consisted of a mosaic of forest and fen, bog and heath bald, canebrake (native cane thickets) and open meadow. The most plentiful tree was the American chestnut, dominating the forest with oaks. Historical records show every fourth tree was a chestnut. Their burred nuts were a plentiful, reliable source of food. Wildlife resembled that of a tableau from Yellowstone National Park. Herds of bison grazed meadows. Elk found pastures in lush bogs and heath balds. White-tailed deer browsed forest edges. Wolves and panthers (mountain lions) stalked grazers. Black bears rummaged among fallen logs.

Overhead, passenger pigeons flew in flocks so huge they darkened the skies. Biologist Alexander Wilson in Kentucky estimated an 1808 flock at 2 1/4 billion birds.

The mountains were the home of thousands of Native Americans. The largest group was the Cherokee Nation, whose settlements ranged from Alabama and Georgia north to Kentucky and Virginia. Others included the Shawnee in West Virginia.

The first European to see the Southern Appalachians was Spanish explorer Hernando DeSoto. He came in 1540 in search of gold. Historical accounts say DeSoto named the mountains after the Appalachee Indians of western Florida.

European settlers began trickling into the region during the 18th Century. Initially, the towering Appalachians acted as a barrier to settlement. Then, in 1775, frontiersman Daniel Boone led pioneers through Cumberland Gap at the juncture of what is now Kentucky, Tennessee and Virginia. Increasing waves of settlers, mostly of English, German and Scotch-Irish descent, moved west as America expanded into Kentucky, Tennessee and West Virginia.

The newcomers' thirst for land coupled with the discovery of gold in northern Georgia in 1828 drove most of the Cherokees from their homelands. President Andrew Jackson in 1838 sent U.S. sol-

Great Smoky Mountains National Park

American chestnut trees, such as these in western North Carolina, once dominated the original forest of the Southern Appalachians.

27

diers to round up 16,000 Cherokees and herd them in a forced march to relocation lands in Oklahoma. About 4,000 died along the way on that infamous "Trail of Tears." Several hundred Cherokees hid out in the mountains of North Carolina, where they ultimately secured a tract of land they called the Qualla Boundary. Their descendants today live on and around that land, at Cherokee, N.C.

As the settlers tamed the vast wilderness, the hoof beats, howls and hisses of wildlife receded.

By the late 1700s, the bison was all but gone. A sign along the Blue Ridge Parkway north of Asheville, N.C., notes the animal's demise: "View Bull Creek Valley. The last buffalo seen in this locality was killed nearby in 1799 by Joseph Rice, an early settler."

The last elk in Tennessee was shot in 1849. In West Virginia, elk survived until about 1870 in remote areas. Wolves and panthers, persecuted as varmints, held on until the early 1900s in the area of the Great Smokies before extirpation.

By the end of the 1800s, most of the Southern Appalachians had been settled. But the highlands remained remote and isolated, speckled with hardscrabble farms.

"Near the turn of the century, the conservation of plants and animals was at a low point for this area. Slash and burn agriculture, willful extermination of species, and a view of the forest as a threat and an impediment to progress often resulted in a devastated landscape," noted the U.S.Forest Service in a 1994 environmental assessment for the Nantahala and Pisgah National Forests in North Carolina.

But mountain after mountain of original forest still stood, a bounty for the taking for those with axes, saws, mule teams, railroads and sawmills. The wholesale cutting of the Southern Appalachian forest was about to begin.

Rebirth and restoration

As the 20th Century began, the Southern Appalachians held some of the last areas of original wilderness in the East.

The old-growth forests drew platoons of loggers from West Virginia to Georgia. With no restraints on timber cutting, the loggers stripped mountain after mountain of trees.

For 30 years the Southern Appalachians suffered massive environmental devastation. Dry debris became fuel for fires ignited by sparks from logging trains. Uncontrolled wildfires burned for weeks. The devastation left the mountains denuded, charred and bereft of most life.

"One series of fires was reported to have burned continuously for nearly two months," wrote Robert S. Lambert in a 1958 report for Great Smoky Mountains National Park; "others burned the sides of such high areas as Clingman's Dome, Siler's Bald and Mount Guyot."

Yet, as the loggers pressed forward, the seeds for a new wilderness already had been planted.

At the turn of the century, virtually all federal lands lay west of the Mississippi River. The East had no national parks or national forests. Conservation-minded individuals led by Dr. Chase P. Ambler of Asheville, N.C., and others revered the beauty of the mountains and deplored the wanton timber cutting. They wanted to carve out an Eastern equivalent of Yellowstone National Park in the North Caro-

U.S. Forest Service

Loggers stripped mountains of trees in the early 1900s; this logging train operated in what is now the Pisgah National Forest in North Carolina.

lina mountains, according to *Mountaineers and Rangers*, a U.S. Forest Service history of the region published in 1983.

The quest for an Appalachian National Park temporarily gave way for a system of "forest reserves" in the region. The concept drew the backing of regional and national timber groups.

But opponents objected to land purchases by the federal government, citing states' rights. Proponents countered that the power of Congress to regulate interstate commerce gave it authority to acquire forest reserves. "The theory ran as follows: Removal of the forest cover affects stream flooding to such an extent that navigation is threatened; restoration of the forest will assure stream control, and hence navigation," according to *Mountaineers and Rangers.*

The legislation nonetheless stalled. It took a disastrous flood to validate the argument for acquiring private lands in the East.

High in the Allegheny Mountains of West Virginia, loggers had left no forest to sop up rainfall. In 1907, spring rains drenched the area. The swollen streams poured their waters into the Monongahela

River, which flows north into western Pennsylvania. The river became a raging torrent, flooding the countryside all the way to Pittsburgh.

"It devastated all the rich agricultural land in the basin of the Monongahela River," noted a 1970 history of the Monongahela National Forest, "causing some $100 million in damages — a gigantic sum for those times — then descending in all its fury upon the helpless city of Pittsburgh, causing there additional damages of $8 million, drowning people and ruining their homes."

The flood prompted Congress in 1911 to pass the Weeks Act. The legislation called for purchase of mountain watersheds to protect the headwaters of navigable streams and to ensure a continuous supply of wood.

The Weeks Act proved profound. It would become the genesis for nearly all the national forests in the East. The first Weeks Act purchase came in 1912. The government bought 8,100 acres near Marion, N.C., for just over $7 an acre. Timber companies, eager to get rid of their logged-over lands, sold them at bargain-basement prices of $5 to $10 an acre.

National forests quickly came into existence. The Pisgah, in North Carolina, began in 1915 with the purchase of 86,700 acres from the estate of millionaire George Vanderbilt. Next, in 1918, came the Shenandoah National Forest in Virginia and West Virginia, now the George Washington National Forest; the Natural Bridge National Forest in Kentucky, Virginia and West Virginia, now the Jefferson National Forest. The Alabama National Forest in Alabama, now the Bankhead National Forest, came about in 1918 as well, assembled from public domain lands that existed before the Weeks Act. Two years later, Congress designated the Nantahala in North Carolina and the Monongahela in West Virginia.

Lowered land prices during the Great Depression made it possible for the government to buy tracts it otherwise could not have afforded. Congress authorized three other national forests in the region in the 1930s: the Talladega in Alabama and the Sumter in South Carolina, both in 1936, and the Daniel Boone in Kentucky in 1937.

In the meantime, Congress in 1926 authorized the region's first two national parks, Great Smokies and Shenandoah.

Overall, the Weeks Act helped create more than 23 million acres in national forests. As The Conservation Foundation concluded in a 1977 report: "The national forests of the East, in the main, were assembled from land that nobody wanted."

A second-growth forest sprang from these rehabilitated lands. Today, the average age of trees on public lands in the Southern Appalachians is 50 to 90 years. Trees of that age produce nuts and acorns and den sites for wildlife.

These older second-growth forests take on some characteristics of an original, old-growth forest. Foresters and biologists caution, however, that appearances can be deceiving. Second-growth trees, because they were generated from trees cut all at once, grow back at an unnatural, uniform rate. A mass cutting lets direct sunlight strike the shaded, damp forest floor. The heat and drying kill plants and moisture-dependent creatures such as salamanders.

A maturing second-growth forest doesn't have the same biological makeup as an original old-growth forest, notes Dr. Robert Zahner, a retired Clemson University forestry professor. Mobile animals such as birds and bears return quickly to a restored forest. But many slow-moving species such as salamanders and plants don't. Woodland salamanders may take decades to replenish their numbers in a new forest — if they can find a protective corridor in which to migrate.

Wildflower populations may take decades before they fully recover, according to "Sustaining Biodiversity in the Southern Appalachians," a 1994 report by The Wilderness Society.

An old-growth forest is one that hasn't been fundamentally altered by humans. In the East, an old-growth forest contains trees of all ages, from saplings to those up to 800 years old, depending on the species. The life span of the Eastern hemlock is 600 to 800 years; the tulip-poplar, 350 to 500 years; the red spruce, more than 400 years.

Biologists say as a forest ages, it provides more niches for life, more places for creatures to hide, a greater diversity of food, an increasing variety of species as well as a greater population of individual species. Bird populations increase with the variety of foliage. Old-growth forests hold 250 to 300 pairs of birds an acre compared to 200 pairs in a younger, mid-successional forest, according to forest ecologist Daniel Boone of The Wilderness Society.

Today, only remnants of old-growth remain in the Southern Appalachians, perhaps several hundred thousand acres. Great Smokies park has the largest amount, more than 100,000 acres. Most pockets of old-growth sit on steep slopes or in gorges, places loggers passed over.

These overlooked remnants, combined with the maturing second-growth forests, would become the crucible for a new wilderness that would emerge on the public lands of the Southern Appalachians.

"Today, the Southern Appalachians testify to the great conservation efforts of the past century," noted "The Southern Appalachian Assessment," the state of the science report. "The land is once again predominantly forested.... Once again, the ecosystems are among the most biologically diverse in the world...."

The new wilderness

The first "wilderness" designated in the United States was Yellowstone National Park.

Congress established Yellowstone in 1872 primarily because of its spectacular geysers and hot springs. Today, the world's first national park, 2.2 million acres of original wilderness, has never been fenced, logged, plowed or mined.

It wasn't until 1924, however, that the nation took its first step toward preserving wilderness for its own sake. In that year, ecologist Aldo Leopold persuaded the Forest Service to carve out a wilderness preserve in New Mexico's Gila National Forest.

The concept of a national wilderness network came about largely through the work of Bob Marshall, a federal official and a founder of The Wilderness Society. Marshall in 1938 proposed setting aside 45 million acres of roadless areas within the contiguous 48 states that could be preserved as wilderness. He got the Forest Service to protect many of these areas as "primitive." Marshall died in 1939 before he could see his dream fully enacted into reality.

The wilderness movement gained momentum after World War II. Led by Howard Zahniser of The Widerness Society, wilderness proponents began drafting legislation to protect the nation's dwindling wild areas.

The first wilderness bill was introduced in 1956 by Sen. Hubert Humphrey, D-Minn., and Rep. John Saylor, R-Pa. Their bill became the basis for the present wilderness system. The proposal ran into widespread opposition from forest products, grazing and mining industries.

After eight years and 66 different versions, President Lyndon Johnson in 1964 signed the Wilderness Act.

With few exceptions, the act banned roads, cabins, developed campsites, logging, mining, motorized vehicles and power boats. Traditional uses such as hiking, hunting, fishing and primitive camping would continue.

The nation's wilderness areas would be drawn from its national forests, national parks and national wildlife refuges. To be eligible, these public lands:

• Must be at least 5,000 acres or must be of such a size that can be maintained practically.

• Must have no permanent man-made inprovements or human habitation.

• Must have outstanding opportunities for solitude or a primitive or unconfined type of recreation.

Land managers would recommend candidates from roadless areas (separate legislation in 1976 would add Bureau of Land Management lands). Congress would designate wilderness areas, giving them an institutional permanence but making their selection subject to politics.

The Wilderness Act instantly designated 54 areas with 14 million acres. Fifty one of the 54 wildernesses were in western states. To the dismay of wilderness proponents, the East got only three areas: Great Gulf in New Hampshire and Linville Gorge and Shining Rock in North Carolina.

Land managers, strictly applying wilderness standards, screened out nearly all roadless areas in the East and declined to study them as possible wilderness. They reasoned that little "pure" wilderness existed in the heavily developed East.

Wilderness proponents saw the "purity" test as an over-zealous betrayal of the intent of the Wilderness Act. They argued that without some flexibility, millions of people in the East would be deprived of nearby wilderness.

Pro-wilderness forces persuaded Congress in 1975 to pass the Eastern Wilderness Act. The act clarified wilderness standards for lands that previously had been logged, farmed or otherwise altered but now possessed wilderness values. The legislation recognized that the moist, mild climate of the East enabled forests in a few decades to recover from previous devastation. Thus, the effect of the 1975 act was that public land in the East could "grow" wilderness if given enough time.

Under the Eastern Wilderness Act, the Forest Service used the following criteria to identify areas eligible to study for wilderness:

• The land is regaining a natural, untrammeled appearance.

• Nature is taking over, muting or wiping out alterations such as roads.

• The location is conducive to wilderness values.

• The area contains no more than a half mile of improved road for each 1,000 acres.

• No more than 15% of the area may have non-native, planted vegetation. This means mainly trees.

• No more that 20% of the area may not have been cut over in the past 10 years.

• The area contains only a few dwellings on private lands. The dwellings must be in a location so they don't impinge on the natural conditions in the wilderness.

The new standards made the second-growth forests of the Southern Appalachians new reservoirs of potential wilderness. The Forest Service in 1977 initiated a second wilderness review of its lands. Roadless Area Review and Evaluation II focused on 62 million acres of roadless areas nationwide. Two years later the review turned up more that 600,000 acres of roadless areas in the 11 national forests of the Southern Appalachians.

This second search for wilderness produced bitter fights. Unlike national parks and national wildlife refuges, the national forests are managed under a "multiple use" principle mandated by Congress. National forests are zoned for logging, wildlife habitat or recreation.

The RARE II reviews became tugs-of-war between wilderness proponents on one side and the timber industry, timber-dependent communities and their residents on the other. Communities feared wilderness would mean loss of jobs and income because designation puts areas off limits to timber cutting.

"On the whole, mountain people oppose more wilderness, especially in the Cherokee (Tennessee) and Chattahoochee (Georgia) forests," said *Mountaineers and Rangers*, the Forest Service history. "Even in North Carolina, where out-of-state interest in RARE II was strongest, about 62% of respondents opposed more wilderness, 32% supported more."

Meanwhile, the National Park Service and the U.S. Fish and Wildlife Service conducted their own roadless area surveys in relative quiet.

By 1997, Congress had designated 47 wilderness areas in the eight Southern Appalachian states, the largest concentration of wilderness east of the Mississippi River. Seven other proposed wildernesses and wilderness study areas awaited possible designation. Combined, the 54 areas cover 1,047,486 acres.

Time capsules for future generations, the wildernesses of the Southern Appalachians preserve magnificent scenery and extraordinary landscapes.

They offer an undisturbed retreat for people who seek solitude. They protect increasingly rare old-growth forests, provide a habitat for deep-forest species such as black bears and serve as core refuges for animals and plants that otherwise could become threatened or endangered. They help keep mountain ecosystems intact.

Wildernesses protect watersheds that supply pure water to downstream users and help prevent downstream flooding. They improve air quality by the filtering action of trees and plants.

Finally, wildernesses act as "living laboratories" for scientific research and as yardsticks to measure the health of the environment and the processes of nature. Without such pristine benchmarks, we can't tell how far we've strayed from nature's standards of purity, biological diversity and ecological integrity.

Wildlife

When Samuel Kercheval reached the Shenandoah Valley in Virginia in the early 1800s, he found a cornucopia of wildlife.

"The buffalo, elk, deer, bear, panthers, wildcat, wolf, fox, beaver, otter and all other kinds of animals, wild fowl, etc., common to the forest countries, were abundantly plentiful," he wrote in 1833.

Many of the animals that Kercheval and others saw in the pre-development Southern Appalachians have disappeared. The buffalo (bison), elk and panthers long have been extirpated. Many other creatures, however, still roam the ridges, coves and stream sides today. Black bear, bobcat, gray fox, opossum, raccoon, red squirrel, red-tailed hawk and weasel can be found throughout the mountains.

Other species, like the wild turkey and white-tailed deer, have bounced back through restorations and natural migration. The beaver, otter and red wolf were killed off but have returned to their native haunts.

The restorations and protective laws have led to a gradual "rewilding" of the Southern Appalachians. Wilderness areas in many cases serve as core habitat for returning species. They play a significant role in helping restored and endangered species recover.

Here are historical descriptions of some of the more prominent animals that help define the Southern Appalachians, both existing and extirpated species as well as two exotics that have become permanently established.

39

Bison

Despite their image as a grazer of the western plains, bison historically ranged the East as far south as Florida.

Bison, commonly called buffalo, could be found in small herds of perhaps several hundred animals. They grazed meadows or small openings in the mountains and foothills, seeking shelter from the summer sun in thickets of native cane.

Hunters quickly slaughtered the slow-moving targets for food, hides and pleasure. Bison may have held on in the Southern Appalachians until as late as 1825. The following account describes the death of a female and calf in West Virginia: "Kellogg (1937) cites Hub Maxwell's account of a cow bison and her calf being found at a deer lick in Webster County about 1825. They were chased with dogs by the settlers and the calf was killed on Valley Fork of Elk River while the cow was followed and finally shot at Valley Head, Randolph County."

Though long extirpated in the East, about 100,000 plains bison today roam public and private lands in western states in a wild or semi-wild state.

Officials at Great Smoky Mountains

Bison once grazed meadows of the Southern Appalachians before hunters extirpated them by the 18th Century.

National Park get periodic inquiries about whether the park will re-introduce bison as part of its mandate to, where feasible, restore na-tive animals.

The park has considered restoration but has ruled it out for the immediate future, according to Joe Abrell, park resource manager. Abrell said the powerful animals are difficult to control and expen-sive to confine.

Black bear

The black bear has become an enduring symbol of wildness in the Southern Appalachians.

Today, perhaps 10,000 bears inhabit the mountains from Georgia to West Virginia. They've prospered largely because of the maturing, second-growth forests on public lands. Older trees provide nuts and acorns for food and den sites for winter.

Bear population densities have generally increased since 1970. The animals reoccupied previous range in the Georgia and North Carolina mountains in the 1970s and 1980s. In the 1990s, bears be-gan dispersing from Virginia and West Virginia in eastern Kentucky.

Two large sanctuaries, Great Smokies park and Shenandoah Na-tional Park, provide core populations protected from hunting.

While Great Smokies park contains the greater number, 400 to 600 bears, Shenandoah represents ideal bear habitat. The park's 80-mile-long boundary with adjacent farmlands make it a sort of bear bed-and-breakfast.

Shenandoah park biologists say the 250 to 300 or so bears shift to farm fields for food when nuts and acorns become scarce, as they do every three or four years as a result of natural cycles.

The black bear is intelligent with a long memory, good eyesight and a keen sense of smell. They spend most of their lives in seclu-sion, eating plants such as squaw root, grasses, berries, grubs, nuts and even animal carcasses. Retreating to a den in winter, bears don't hibernate but go into a state of lethargy. Adult black bears weigh from 100 to 400 pounds. Males grow larger than females.

Though it's rare to spot a bear, except in national parks, it's easy

Bill Lea

Black bears range throughout most of the Southern Appalachians; this bear lives in Great Smokies park.

to spot bear sign. Look for tracks on muddy parts of trails and scratch marks on trees or wooden trail posts. They also snap off saplings, usually at a height of three to four feet, perhaps as a warning to intruder bears, according to Dr. Michael Pelton, a black bear expert at the University of Tennessee.

Black bears pose little threat to people. Still, here are some tips to avoid any conflicts:

• Keep your food out of reach of bears. Tie a line between two trees and suspend your food from the line. Remember, bears can climb trees.

• Don't approach a wild bear. If you come across a bear on the trail, stop or step behind a tree. If the bear keeps coming, give it room to pass.

• If the bear seems to threaten you, wave your hands and yell. That should scare it off. The bear probably doesn't want to hurt you; it just wants to get on its way.

Brook trout

The only trout native to the Southern Appalachians is the brook trout, found from Labrador to Georgia.

A kind of char, the brook trout evolved into a freshwater fish after its ancestors were trapped inland after sea levels retreated.

They reach lengths of up to 18 inches. They are also called speckled trout after the greenish spots on their back and sides.

Brook trout thrived in the cold-water streams of the mountains until massive logging in the early 1900s devastated much of their habitat. Woody debris and mud choked the streams while cutting of stream-side trees allowed sunlight to warm the water.

As brook trout declined, wildlife officials stocked streams with brown trout from Germany and rainbow trout from western states so sport fishing could resume. Both are bigger, hardier and more aggressive than brook trout.

In Great Smokies park, brown and rainbows invaded 70% of the former range of the brook trout as a result of stocking that continued into the 1950s.

Today, Smokies park officials are trying to undo the damage by removing rainbows and restoring brook trout to streams.

The brook trout is more abundant in Virginia and West Virginia.

Coyote

Coyotes, a native of western states, are among the most recent migrants to the Southern Appalachians.

Coyotes have been moving eastward for decades. They're filling niche created by the elimination of the wolf, occupying the farm-and-forest checkerboard of the Southeast.

They've also had help hopscotching the continent. Unscrupulous hunters buy coyotes in the West and illegally import them into the Southeast for sport. Invariably, some animals escape from their pens and make a new home in the wild.

Coyotes weigh from 20 to 50 pounds, making them larger than foxes and smaller than red wolves. Coyotes eat most anything they can find, from insects to watermelons to rabbits.

During the 1970s and 1980s, coyotes reached the Southern Appalachians and are expected to continue their eastern movement from West Virginia to Georgia.

Elk

The Southern Appalachians once resounded with the bugling and bleating of the North American elk.

Weighing from 600 to 1,000 pounds and grazing mostly on grasses, the animals roamed the mountains and upper foothills when the settlers arrived.

"These beasts are plentifully to be met with in the Savannas near the Mountains and Heads of Rivers," wrote John Brickell in 1737 in *The Natural History of North-Carolina.*

Easy targets for hunters, elk or wapiti began to disappear in the 1700s. One of six races of elk, the eastern elk became extinct by the early 1800s.

Elk became the first extirpated animal returned to the Southern Appalachians. In 1917, Virginia imported about 150 elk from Yellowstone National Park and released them in the Mount Rogers area.

The animals prospered for three decades. In the late 1950s, elk

Elk like this one in Yellowstone National Park await restoration to parts of the Southern Appalachians.

numbers began to drop from hunting pressure. Farmers complained the elk were eating their crops and, in response, game officials lengthened the hunting season. By 1974, the last elk was gone.

West Virginia in 1972 studied the feasibility of stocking elk but dropped the idea. Since, Arkansas, Michigan and Pennsylvania have reestablished elk drawn from western herds that now number nearly one million animals. In 1996, Canadian elk were released in Land Between the Lakes in Kentucky and Tennessee.

Elk again may soon return to the Southern Appalachians. A 1996 proposal by the Forest Service, the N.C. Wildlife Resources Commission and the Rocky Mountain Elk Foundation would release 15 to 20 elk in the Pisgah National Forest near Shining Rock and Middle Prong wilderness areas. The release would be an experiment to determine if a permanent herd could be reestablished.

A University of Tennessee study in 1996 determined sufficient habitat exists in Great Smokies park for more than 50 elk.

One historical deterrent to elk restoration in the East has been the presence of a small brain parasite carried by white-tailed deer. Elk ingest the parasite as they graze. While the parasite doesn't harm deer, it can make elk go crazy and eventually kill them.

Biologist Bob Long, who conducted the habitat study for Great Smokies park, says the threat to elk from the parasite is overstated. He said the annual death rate from the parasite is one elk in every 100.

Fisher

A weasel-like animal, the fisher once hunted in the high-elevation hardwood and conifer forests of the Southern Appalachians.

The fisher, weighing from four to nearly 10 pounds, was trapped for its silky brown fur. By the 19th Century, trapping had eliminated the fisher from the Southern mountains.

The animal now can be found from northern West Virginia to New England and west to California. Fishers prey on snowshoe hares, ruffed grouse, mice, voles, and squirrels.

Fishers could return to Great Smokies park. A proposal by Dr.

Michael Pelton and Bob Long at the University of Tennessee, calls for an experimental release of 10 to 15 fishers to verify that suitable habitat exists.

Restoring fishers could create problems for an endangered species the park must protect. The endangered species is the Carolina northern flying squirrel, natural prey for fishers.

Pelton and Long, however, don't think fishers could harm the squirrel population. They contend that the two animals evolved together without causing the extinction of the squirrel. They suspect that the fisher could actually benefit the flying squirrel. The fisher also preys on the abundant red squirrel, which often kills and eats the young of the smaller flying squirrel.

Panther

The panther, or mountain lion, once prowled the forests of the Southern Appalachians.

The tawny, long-tailed cats weighing from 75 to as much as 200 pounds are known as panthers in the South; mountain people often call them "painters."

Panthers began to disappear in the 1800s. The last reported kill in Kentucky occurred in 1863. In West Virginia, the last known big cat was killed in 1887 near the present Cranberry Wilderness. In 1920, a panther was shot in western North Carolina near the edge of what is now Great Smokies park.

Though it's still a federal endangered species, the eastern race of the mountain lion is believed to be extinct in its former range from eastern Canada south to North Carolina and Tennessee.

Still, sightings continue to roll in, some from credible sources. In 1975, a group of maintenance workers in the Great Smokies park said they saw a long-tailed cat spring from the forest in pursuit of deer.

Robert Downing of the Fish and Wildlife Service investigated the panther-sighting phenomenon in the 1980s. He tracked down dozens of sightings and even inspected a dead "panther" (it was a large house cat). But Downing could find no evidence of any wild population.

The most plausible explanation: People buy young western cougars to raise as pets. The animals grow into adults, become too difficult to keep and are dumped into the wild.

The only known wild panthers in the Southeast are the 30 to 50 Florida panthers that live in south Florida. To help promote the recovery of this endangered species, the Fish and Wildlife Service wants to reestablish populations outside south Florida.

The service evaluated 14 candidate sites in Florida and elsewhere in the Southeast for possible restoration of Florida panthers. The 14 sites include a 7,621-square-mile area in the Southern Appalachians in North Carolina, Tennessee and Georgia, including Great Smokies park and surrounding national forests.

The 1994 report by Dennis Jordan, the Florida panther coordinator, preliminarily ranked the Southern Appalachian Mountains site as eighth in desirability, based in part on forest cover, human population and density of roads.

Jim Reed, Florida Game & Fresh Water Fish Commission

The closest relative of the native panther of the Southern Appalachians, this Florida panther roams wild lands of southern Florida.

Ken Taylor, N.C. Wildlife Resources Commission

Reintroduced peregrine falcon find homes in wilderness areas like Linville Gorge and Shenandoah National Park.

Peregrine falcon

Soaring high above their nests on mountain cliffs, the peregrine falcon has resumed its role as a long-time resident of the Southern Appalachians.

The falcon is a medium-sized hawk with pointed wings and long tail. It's agile in flight and can reach speeds of up to 200 miles an hour when it dives for prey, primarily other birds.

In the 1950s, the falcon population plummeted because of the pesticide DDT. DDT caused egg shells to become thin and crack, resulting in the death of the unborn chicks. By 1965, the peregrine falcon had become extirpated from the East as a breeding population.

The ban of DDT in 1972 paved the way for the raptor's return through captive breeding and restorations in the wild. Falcons once again glide about the East. While the eastern race became extinct, a hybrid mix of western birds and European birds has taken its place.

Restorations in the East began in 1984. In North Carolina, the first pair of falcons were released in 1986 in Linville Gorge Wilderness. The bird also has been released in Great Smokies park, Shenandoah National Park and Southern Nantahala Wilderness.

By 1997, more than 350 peregrines had been hatched in six mountain states from West Virginia to South Carolina and Tennessee. About 12 pairs now live in the Southern Appalachians, according to the Fish and Wildlife Service.

The agency in 1995 took initial steps to remove the peregrine falcon from the endangered species list as populations approached 1,000 nesting pairs in the 48 contiguous states.

Red wolf

The early settlers treated wolves as vermin, offering bounties for their scalps.

The last wolves were killed in the Southern Appalachians between 1900 and 1910, according to various accounts. A straggler was killed in North Carolina in 1933, near what is now Middle Prong and Shining Rock wildernesses.

The Southern Appalachians may have been part of the range of both the red wolf and the gray wolf, separate species. Though the gray wolf may never return, Great Smokies park began restoring the red wolf in 1991.

The red wolf is the native wolf of the Southeast, weighing from 40 to 80 pounds. The animals have tawny or cinnamon coats. They hunt alone, with a mate or in small family groups, chasing down rabbits, raccoons and deer.

The red wolf faced extinction in the early 1970s. To save the

Barron Crawford, U.S. Fish and Wildlife Service

This red wolf, wearing a radio collar around its neck, stalks prey in Great Smoky Mountains National Park.

species, the Fish and Wildlife Service from 1974 through 1979 trapped 400 wolf-like animals in Louisiana and Texas. Sorting out coyote-wolf hybrids, biologists found just 14 pure red wolves.

The 14 became the founding fathers and mothers for captive breeding programs that produced today's restored wolves.

In 1987, the Fish and Wildlife Service first restored red wolves to the 150,000-acre Alligator River National Wildlife Refuge in coastal North Carolina.

Later, the 520,000-acre Smokies park was considered a promising restoration site because of its size and adjoining national forest lands. A permanent population of 75 to 100 wolves was envisioned.

So far, 37 wolves have been released, all on the Tennessee side of the park. Of these, 10 have died. A poacher shot and killed an 18-month-old female in 1995 near Deals Gap on the North Carolina side of the park. As of 1997, nine adult wolves ranged the park. One had found a home in the nearby Joyce Kilmer-Slickrock Wilderness.

Six years after the first release, biologists have concluded the park may support only a few wolves because of low densities of prey animals except in places like the meadows and fields of Cades Cove.

A study is underway to determine whether better habitat exists on national forest lands or other federal lands.

White-tailed deer

It's hard to imagine that white-tailed deer were scarce animals as recently as the 1930s and 1940s in the Southern Appalachians.

Deer had been wiped out in much of the Southeast because of unregulated hunting and widespread conversion of forests to farms and pastures.

Today, deer have recovered to the point that they number in the hundreds of thousands per state and have become pests in some areas. In North Carolina, for example, deer numbers rose from 10,000 in 1900 to an estimated one million in 1997, according to the state Wildlife Resources Commission.

Nationally, the white-tailed deer population has been estimated at more than 14 million animals, probably more than existed 400 years ago.

The chance of seeing deer while on a hike in a Southern Appalachian wilderness is high. Everyone gets a thrill hearing a deer's warning cough, the clatter of hoofs on the forest floor and, perhaps, glimpsing a flash of its upturned white tail.

Wild hog

A mostly nocturnal, rarely seen exotic in the Southern Appalachians is the wild hog.

The wild hog is an example of an invading species that found a hospitable niche and, in the absence of natural predators, adapted to a new home.

Wild hogs trace their origin to 13 European wild boar imported in 1912 to a private game preserve in Western North Carolina. A few of the animals escaped through the fence surrounding the preserve and bred with domestic hogs.

By 1940 hybrid hog had made its way into the western side of Great Smokies park. It moved eastward in the 1950s and 1960s. Today, a few hundred to 1,000 live in the park, not counting those in nearby national forests in North Carolina, Tennessee and Georgia.

The National Park Service regards the animal as a destructive pest. Hogs root up rare wild flowers, wallow in springs and compete with native animals such as bears for nuts and other food.

Park officials have tried to rid Great Smokies of hogs for several decades by trapping and shooting. But they only have been able to hold down hog numbers and check their spread into some areas.

Wild hogs have long snouts with broad shoulders and narrow hips covered with coarse hair. The males weigh about 150 pounds, although some animals grow to as large as 400 pounds. Adults have sharp, curved tusks two to four inches long, used for slashing their attackers. While adults are dark gray, the young have stripes that resemble the markings of chipmunks.

Despite their fierce appearance, wild hogs pose little danger to hikers. The animals will flee at the slightest sound or sight of an intruder. If cornered, however, they will stand and even attack.

Pests and pollution

The demise of the king of the Southern Appalachian forest, the American chestnut tree, began in the 1920s.

Chestnuts began dying from an invisible, airborne blight accidentally imported from Asia. The blight swept through the Southern Appalachians by the 1940s and 1950s, killing millions of trees.

The loss was catastrophic. Each tree annually produced hundreds, perhaps thousands of burred nuts that animals like black bears and wild turkeys relied on for food. Farmers would turn loose livestock to fatten on the nuts. Today, only split-rail fences, decaying logs and rotting stumps remain to remind us of the magnificent tree.

The chestnut could come back. Live shoots still rise from chestnut stumps, though the blight kills them back before they're more than three to four feet high. Scientists hope the combination of live rootstock, an occasional tree that managed to survive and the Asian chestnut will give them the ingredients to produce both a blight-resistant chestnut and an anti-blight virus to inoculate living chestnut roots.

The chestnut blight was among the first of a seemingly never-ending parade of diseases, insect pests and pollutants to beset the Southern Appalachian forests. All told, they've caused widespread damage to mountain forests. The worst may yet come.

A 1994 report by the Virginia Division of Natural Heritage summed up forest problems this way: "Appalachian forests in particular are being besieged by an ever-growing number of natural and anthropogenic (human-caused) perturbations and threats. Already, a keystone tree species, the American chestnut (*Castanea dentata*), has been virtually eliminated due to an introduced fungal pathogen."

The report said other native trees including eastern hemlock, butternut, dogwood, red spruce and several oaks are in decline because of the direct or suspected synergistic influences of insects, diseases and environmental contamination.

Two years later, a state of the science report described the disease, pest and pollution problems in detail. Here is a synopsis from that 1996 report, "The Southern Appalachian Assessment."

Balsam woolly adelgid

First detected on Mount Mitchell in North Carolina in 1957, the pest has devastated Fraser fir trees throughout their range. The pest kills trees after they mature and bear seeds, thus allowing reproduction of new trees. Control efforts to reduce the spread of the adelgid, accidentally imported from Europe, have failed. Great Smoky Mountains National Park preserves some of its firs with repeated sprayings of a soapy solution, a costly process.

Beech bark disease

The combination of beech scale insects and a fungus prove fatal for the American beech. The disease has been found in the Monongahela National Forest and Great Smokies park since the 1980s.

Butternut canker

In three decades this fungus has killed 90 percent of the butternut trees in the Southern Appalachians. Some surviving butternuts may carry genetic resistance to the disease.

Dogwood anthracnose

Detected in the 1970s, this disease infects the eastern flowering dogwood and has spread across 12 million acres in the East. Dogwoods usually die in two to three years. No practical controls are available for trees in forest environments. Dogwood berries provide a high-energy food source for many species of birds.

Dutch elm disease

This fungus was introduced into the United States in 1930. American elm is slowly declining in forest stands but the disease is not an immediate threat to the species.

Gypsy moth

A European insect that came to this country in the 1860s, the gypsy moth defoliated about 36 million acres of trees between 1982 and 1992. The moth, which prefers oak leaves, is expected to spread from Virginia south to North Carolina, Tennessee and Georgia in the next few years. Most trees recover without dying. A fungus, Entomophaga maimaiga, has proved to be effective at killing the moth caterpillars.

Hemlock woolly adelgid

Another imported native of Asia, the adelgid infests Eastern and Carolina hemlock trees. Once weakened, the trees lose their foliage and can't produce cones. Unless treated, scientists say it appears hemlocks may be doomed because there's no known genetic resistance.

Oak decline

This is a disease complex involving stresses such as drought, root disease and insect pests in mature trees. Oak decline is a natural ecosystem process, affecting about 19 percent of oaks on national forest land in the Southern Appalachians.

Spruce decline

Decline of red spruce has been reported in the Northeast since the early 1980s. Detection of spruce decline in the Southern Appalachians is difficult since the tree coexists with Fraser firs. The structure of spruce-fir forests in most areas has deteriorated since the early 20th Century due to logging and infestation of the fir by the balsam woolly adelgid. In mixed stands with dying fir, spruce decline can be partially explained by increases in wind damage and warmer soil temperatures. The dead trees, shorn of their needles, allow additional sunlight to hit the soil.

Visibility deterioration

Over the past 40 years, visibility in the Southern Appalachians has been degraded. The culprit is primarily sulfur from the burning of coal and oil. Sulfur forms sulfate aerosols, which create haze that scatters light. This reduces visibility. The annual visibility distance in the Southern Appalachians has dropped to 20 miles. Visibility is expected to improve by three to seven miles after the year 2000, when sulfur dioxide reductions for coal-burning power plants required by the Clean Air Act Amendments of 1990 have taken place.

Ozone damage

Ozone is formed from the chemical reaction of nitrogen oxides and volatile organic compounds released from auto exhaust and industrial plants. Ground-level ozone, when soil moisture is adequate to increase the uptake of ozone in trees and plants, may be sufficient to cause growth losses to the most sensitive species. Great Smokies park has reported symptoms of ozone injury to 21 trees, 15 herbs, 9 shrubs, three vines, one fern and one grass species.

Acid precipitation

Acid rain, snow and cloud water formed from sulfate and nitrate pollutants threaten soil, water and forests. Great Smokies park in 1993 recorded the highest sulfate and nitrate deposition in the Southeast. Deposition is even greater on the high-elevation peaks because of pollutants released in cloud water. In the mid-Appalachian region, about 30 percent of target stream reaches are likely to become acidic during the worst rainfall episodes.

A consequence of this increased, unnatural acidity is the possibility of injury to trees. Research has suggested that acidity releases aluminum in the soil, which blocks the uptake of calcium and magnesium that trees need to make cells. The loss of these elements may weaken trees and perhaps make them vulnerable to insects or disease.

The danger of continued acidification of streams is that it could eliminate aquatic life, including fish. In the Saint Mary's River in Virginia, the number and diversity of aquatic insects decreased between 1936 and 1988, an indication of acidification. In Shenandoah National Park, researchers studying three streams have found chronic and episodic exposures to acidity have caused lethal and sub-lethal effects on fish, particularly brook trout and the blacknose dace.

In summary, according to The Southern Appalachian Assessment, "The northern portion of the Southern Appalachians in West Virginia and in Virginia appears to be exposed to higher concentrations of pollutants which affect natural resources. Visibility

Dead Fraser firs in Great Smoky Mountains National Park illustrate damage from pests and pollution in the Southern Appalachian forests.

is worse in these areas; the frequency of ground-level ozone damage is likely to be greater; acid deposition is higher; and the soils have low buffering capacity, so adverse effects are more likely. This pattern is also true for visibility and potential damage from ozone in the southern portion of the assessment area in northern Georgia and Alabama."

Part 2

Wilderness Profiles

Wilderness Profiles

The following chapters profile the 54 wildernesses, proposed wildernesses and wilderness study areas of the Southern Appalachians.

The profiles are listed alphabetically by state, from Alabama to West Virginia.

Wildernesses that lie in two states fall under the state that has the greater acreage. Ellicott Rock Wilderness in Georgia, North Carolina and South Carolina is listed under South Carolina even though the North Carolina section has the greatest acreage. The reason: Most people (90 percent) enter from the South Carolina side.

Some profiles combine two wildernesses. Wildernesses that adjoin or lie across a road from each other are described in a single profile. Locater maps accompanying profiles should not be used for hiking.

At the end of each profile is an information summary. Here is a guide to each entry.

• "Size" refers to the actual acreage measured after wilderness designation. This number may disagree with the figure published in Congressional bills.

• "Year designated' and "years designated" refer to the years that Congress approved wilderness designation and any subsequent additions.

• "Public land unit" refers to either the Forest Service or the National Park Service.

• "Features" refers to prominent landforms or landmarks that distinguish the wilderness.

• "Representative wildlife" refers to animals that may be characteristic of the wilderness.

• "Wilderness maps" refers to individual maps published by the Forest Service or the Park Service.

The Forest Service publishes wilderness maps for most but not all areas. The maps, however, vary in format, detail and cost from state to state and from wilderness to wilderness.

The agency provides full-color, topographic-scale maps of 12 wildernesses. They are Cheaha, Citico Creek-Joyce Kilmer-Slickrock, Beaver Creek-Clifty, Cohutta, Ellicott Rock, Lewis Fork-Little Wilson Creek (under the name Mount Rogers High Country), Linville Gorge, Middle Prong-Shining Rock, Ramsey's Draft, Saint Mary's and Southern Nantahala. The scale for these maps is 1:24,000, with elevation contours either every 40 feet or every 100 feet. This is the same scale as the standard U.S. Geological Survey topographic quadrangle maps. The Forest Service maps cost about $4 and are available from the agency or at most outdoor shops.

Maps for most other wildernesses consist of black-and-white brochures or single page maps. Usually free, these maps contain less detail. There are no maps for several wilderness areas in the Chattahoochee, Cherokee and Monongahela forests. In those instances, visitors should use forest-wide maps. These full-color forest maps carry a scale of 1:126,720. That's about a fifth of the 1:24,000-scale wilderness maps. The forest maps do not contain elevation contour lines. Newer wilderness areas may not be marked.

Detailed maps for Cumberland Gap National Historical Park, Great Smoky Mountains National Park and Shenandoah National Park are available from the parks and from outdoor stores.

Hiking guidebooks carry maps and trail descriptions of most wilderness areas. A state-by-state list appears in the Appendix.

"U.S.G.S. topographic maps" refers to the U.S. Geological Survey topographic maps with 1:24,000 scale. They are available at most outdoor stores or map shops.

"Information" refers to the addresses and phone numbers of the appropriate Forest Service or National Park Service office.

Wilderness areas are part of the nation's public lands. They are open to non-vehicular recreation. That includes hiking, overnight camping, rock climbing, fishing, snowshoeing and cross-country skiing. Hunting is allowed in national forests but not in national parks. Horse riding is allowed on some trails in some wildernesses. Permits may be required for some activities.

Wilderness may not be for everyone. Entering a wilderness entails a certain level of risk.

Visitors should understand these areas are among the most remote and most isolated parts of the Southern Appalachians. The roads leading to the wilderness boundary often are dirt logging roads. Such roads may be impassable during rain and snow. Four-wheel-drive vehicles may be required. It's prudent to start with a full tank of gas before searching for an unfamiliar wilderness.

Wilderness areas, by design, don't have well-developed and well-marked trails. Painted slash marks on trees and rocks that serve as guideposts for trails in national forests do not exist in most wildernesses. The Appalachian Trail is an exception.

Expect trails to be minimal, occasionally overgrown footpaths. Expect to ford streams. Always carry a compass or a global positional systems receiver, extra water and food and emergency equipment that includes waterproof matches, a flashlight and a foil blanket. Be prepared to spend the night if you lose your way.

To reduce visitation and impact on wilderness areas, consider hiking in semi-primitive, non-motorized areas. These are sometimes called backcountry areas. These areas contain many characteristics of wilderness areas.

Remember to observe wilderness ethics. Stay on trails, use portable stoves instead of wood for fires and pack out what you pack in. Don't pick wildflowers. Consider hiking during the week to avoid weekend crowds. Minimize your impact on wilderness.

Designated and proposed wilderness areas

AREA	STATUS	ACRES
Alabama		
Cheaha	Wilderness	7,297
Sipsey	Wilderness	25,002
Georgia		
Blood Mountain	Wilderness	7,800
Brasstown	Wilderness	12,975
Cohutta *	Wilderness	36,977
Mark Trail	Wilderness	16,400
Raven Cliffs	Wilderness	9,115
Rich Mountain	Wilderness	9,649
Tray Mountain	Wilderness	9,702
Kentucky		
Beaver Creek	Wilderness	4,791
Clifty	Wilderness	12,646
Cumberland Gap Park *	Proposed	6,375
North Carolina		
Craggy Mountain	Study area	2,380
Great Smokies Park *	Proposed	466,000
Harper Creek	Study area	7,140
Joyce Kilmer-Slickrock *	Wilderness	17,394
Linville Gorge	Wilderness	12,002
Lost Cove	Study area	5,710
Middle Prong	Wilderness	7,460
Overflow	Study area	3,200

Shining Rock	Wilderness	18,483
Snowbird	Study area	8,490
Southern Nantahala *	Wilderness	23,714
South Carolina		
Ellicott Rock *	Wilderness	8,274
Tennessee		
Bald River Gorge	Wilderness	3,721
Big Frog *	Wilderness	8,082
Big Laurel Branch	Wilderness	6,332
Citico Creek	Wilderness	16,226
Gee Creek	Wilderness	2,493
Little Frog Mountain	Wilderness	4,666
Pond Mountain	Wilderness	6,929
Sampson Mountain	Wilderness	7,992
Unaka Mountain	Wilderness	4,496
Virginia		
Barbours Creek	Wilderness	5,382
Beartown	Wilderness	5,609
James River Face	Wilderness	8,886
Kimberling Creek	Wilderness	5,542
Lewis Fork	Wilderness	5,618
Little Dry Run	Wilderness	2,858
Little Wilson Creek	Wilderness	3,613
Mountain Lake *	Wilderness	11,113
Peters Mountain	Wilderness	3,328
Ramseys Draft	Wilderness	6,518
Rich Hole	Wilderness	6,450
Rough Mountain	Wilderness	9,300
Saint Mary's	Wilderness	9,835
Shawvers Run	Wilderness	3,467
Shenandoah Park	Wilderness	79,579
Thunder Ridge	Wilderness	2,344
West Virginia		
Cranberry	Wilderness	35,864
Dolly Sods	Wilderness	10,215
Laurel Fork North	Wilderness	6,055
Laurel Fork South	Wilderness	5,997
Otter Creek	Wilderness	20,000

TOTAL   **1,047,486**

* Area located in two or more states.

Wilderness, proposed wilderness and wilderness study areas of the Southern Appalachians

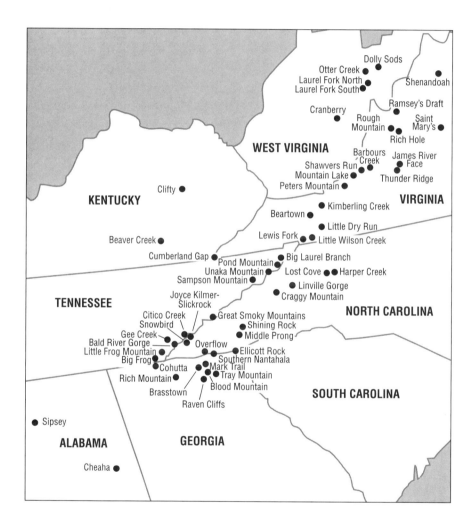

Those were the days when all the soil was virgin. The woods were full of wild peas on which the hogs fattened. So big were the trees then, so far did the forest stretch, that it was more than a man could do to clear his land with an ax. He had to girdle the trees, and let them die; then he burned them down, with the result that a pioneer cabin was usually surrounded by desolate-looking silvered trees, and the air was often filled with a pall of smoke. Still, all the streams ran clear, and you could drink anywhere. A barrel of fish could be captured overnight in the rushing streams. Beyond the mountain, adventure beckoned always.

— Donald Culross Peattie, describing the mountain settlements of the 18th Century, in *The Great Smokies and the Blue Ridge/The Story of the Southern Appalachians*, edited by Roderick Peattie, The Vanguard Press, New York, 1943.

ALABAMA

Cheaha Wilderness

Cheaha is the southernmost mountain wilderness in the Southeast, a distant island at the end of the Southern Appalachian range.

Cheaha has been carved out of the Talladega Mountains in east-central Alabama. The Talladegas, 1,100 to 2,400 feet high, are relative hills compared to the 6,000-foot-high peaks of North Carolina, Tennessee and Virginia.

But the difference in elevation from the surrounding land to the summits gives visitors a feeling of breathtaking height.

Cheaha, pronounced chee-HAW, is a wilderness that almost wasn't. In the 1970s, the state proposed extending the Talladega Scenic Drive southward across the peaks that make up Cheaha. But wilderness advocates fought for an alternate, less environentally damaging route west of the wilderness.

In 1983, Congress created Cheaha Wilderness, permanently protecting about 6,600 acres in the Talladega National Forest. In 1988, Congress added 753 acres. (Later surveys put Cheaha's size at 7,297 acres).

The Cheaha area was the setting for early 19th Century battles in the Creek Indian Wars. Federal troops led by Gen. Andrew Jackson, who later became president, fought the Creeks in 1813-14. The wars ended with the Battle of Horseshoe Bend with the defeat of the Creek nation.

The wilderness is named for the adjacent Cheaha Mountain, at 2,407 feet the highest point in Alabama. Cheaha is an Indian word for high. The mountain is part of Cheaha State Park, whose 2,719 acres adjoin the wilderness on its northern border.

The wilderness blends the craggy geology of more northern mountains with the vegetation of the Alabama Piedmont. Granite and quartz outcroppings, cliffs and rock slides mark the higher elevations. Virginia pines, sweet birch and chestnut oaks make up much of the forest. Wild blueberry and wild hydrangea compete for a place in the sun.

At the summits, stunted Virginia pine among the rock outcrops give the appearance of a giant bonsai garden. Maples and hardwood shrubs are found along high elevation ridges.

The wilderness contains the headwaters of several streams, including the Cheaha, Ketchepedrake and Talladega creeks. The small, clear streams tumble across the ridges, under gnarled stands of mountain laurel. Cinnamon and royal ferns live in wet areas.

Quiet hikers can spot white-tailed deer, oppossum or perhaps a wild turkey. Bird watchers find a wide variety of songbirds in Cheaha. They range from Eastern bluebirds to black-throated green warblers to indigo buntings.

The 105-mile-long Pinhoti Trail spans 8.1 miles of Cheaha, from Cheaha State Park on the northern boundary to Adams Gap on the western boundary. It's marked with a white, turkey-foot blaze. Overall, Cheaha has three trails totalling 21.7 miles.

Work is underway to link the Pinhoti Trail to the Benton MacKaye Trail in north Georgia. The Benton MacKaye Trail ties into the Appalachian Trail at Georgia's Springer Mountain. Once completed, Cheaha will be the southern terminus of a trail system that runs from Alabama to Maine.

Cheaha Wilderness lies about 25 miles south of Anniston and about 65 miles east of Birmingham.

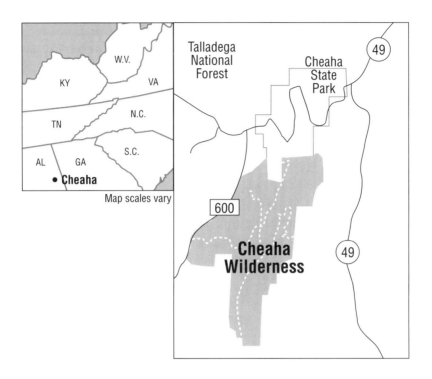

CHEAHA WILDERNESS
Size: 7,297 acres.
Years designated: 1983, 1988.
Public land unit: Talladega National Forest.
Features: Craggy, rock-strewn mountains with vistas of the Talladega Mountains.
Representative wildlife: White-tailed deer, gray fox, big brown bat.
Wilderness map: The 1:24,000-scale Cheaha Wilderness map (does not include 1988 expansion of 723 acres.)
U.S.G.S. topographic maps: Cheaha Mountain; Ironaton; Lineville West.
County: Clay.
Information: Talladega Ranger District, 1001 North Street, Talladega, AL 35160. (205) 362-2909; Heflin Ranger District, 450 Highway 46, Heflin, AL 36264. (205) 463-2272.

Sipsey Wilderness

A crystal-clear river, cascading waterfalls, steep canyons and groves of individual large hemlocks and oaks make Sipsey a wilderness gem in the Alabama foothills.

73

A naturalist's delight, Sipsey contains a wide diversity of species that spring from the convergence of cool and warm, wet and dry ecosystems. It lies at the juncture of three geologic areas: the Appalachian Plateau; the Cumberland plateau and the Coastal Plain.

Sipsey's original forest soon yielded to farms and settlements in the mid-1800s. Between 1875 and 1915 most of the land now covered by the wilderness had been transformed into homesteads. The homesteading, however, was short lived. A combination of thin soils and poor agricultural practices led to an abandonment of many farms beginning in the late 1800s.

Today, the wilderness contains old-growth stands of yellow poplar in the Bee Branch area. Among the trees is the so-called "Champion Poplar," the largest tree in Alabama. The massive tree, with a 22-foot circumference, is 300 years or older.

Sipsey, at 25,002 acres, is part of the Bankhead National Forest in northwest Alabama. The wilderness could have been even larger. A 1980 House bill would have expanded Sipsey to 40,000 acres but the bill died in the Senate.

The core of Sipsey was the former Bee Branch Scenic Area, 1,200 acres of canyons and gorges that had been protected administratively by the Forest Service.

The move to create a wilderness began in 1969 by the Alabama Conservancy. But the Forest Service, applying strict "purity' standards drawn from the 1964 Wilderness Act, concluded in 1971 that the human imprint was too great to qualify Bee Branch for wilderness.

Wilderness designation came, however, in 1975 when Congress enacted the Eastern Wilderness Act. Sipsey's original size of 12,726 acres was expanded in 1988 to its present size.

The 1988 legislation that expanded Sipsey also established a National Wild and Scenic River along the West Fork of the Sipsey River, which flows through the wilderness. The 62-mile-long wild and scenic river also includes several major tributaries, including Borden and Thompson creeks.

The scenic river corridor protects 4,590 adjacent acres on northern and southern borders of the wilderness.

The river's deep enough for canoes yet shallow enough most of the year for fording by hikers, depending on rainfall.

Water has carved steep canyons through Sipsey's major streams, revealing sculptured sandstone rocks, cave-like overhangs and occasional waterfalls. Cliffs may approach 75 feet high or more. At the bottom of the canyons, huge boulders lie strewn on the sandy stream bed.

The river itself winds like a jade ribbon through the canyons, making a few riffles here and there and creating limpid pools for redeyed bass. The elevation in the wilderness descends from a high of 1,022 feet in the northwest corner to 560 feet at the point where the Sipsey River leaves the wilderness.

Eastern hemlocks and American beech border the river in places,

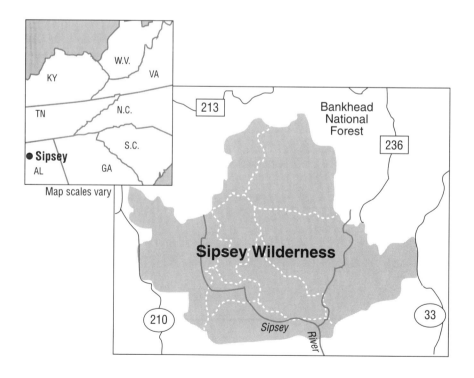

part of the scattered patches of individual old-growth trees. Sandstone outcroppings hanging over the trees made it impractical for loggers to get the trees out of the canyons and gorges.

The forest floor harbors wildflowers such as wild azalea, violets, wild flox and trilliums.

Visitors may see white-tailed deer, wild turkey and other small mammals and songbirds. The wilderness is within the Black Warrior Wildlife Management Area.

Sipsey has about 25 miles of maintained trails. Several trails cross the Sipsey River; be prepared to wade the river for the wilderness has no bridges.

The wilderness is about 40 miles southwest of Decatur in the northwestern part of the state.

SIPSEY WILDERNESS
Size: 25,002 acres.
Years designated: 1975, 1988.
Public land unit: Bankhead National Forest.
Features: Steep canyons, rocky overhangs, boulder-strewn streams.
Representative wildlife: White-tailed deer, wild turkey, redeye bass.
Wilderness map: The 1:63,360-scale Sipsey Wilderness map.
U.S.G.S. topographic maps: Bee Branch; Grayson; Kinlock Spring; Landersville.
Counties: Lawrence; Winston.
Information: Bankhead Ranger District, Box 278, Double Springs, AL 35553. (205) 489-5111.

Massive boulders embellish Sipsey River in Sipsey Wilderness.

Of these (passenger pigeons) there come in winter to Virginia and Carolina, from the North, incredible numbers; insomuch that in some places where they roost (which they do on one another's backs) they often break down the limbs of oaks with their weight and leave their dung some inches thick on the trees they roost on. Where they light, they so effectually clear the woods of acorns and other mast, that the hogs that come after them, to the detriment of the planters, fare very poorly. In Virginia I have seen them fly in such continued trains three days successively, that there was not the least interval in losing sight of them, but that somewhere or other in the air they were to be seen continuing their flight south.

—Naturalist Mark Catesby, describing passenger pigeons in the early 1700s. From *Catesby's Birds of Colonial America*, edited by Alan Feduccia, 1985, University of North Carolina Press, Chapel Hill and London.

GEORGIA

Big Frog Wilderness

See Tennessee section for a description of Big Frog Wilderness.

Blood Mountain Wilderness

This wilderness draws its name from Blood Mountain, a 4,458-foot-high peak studded with rock outcrops and old-growth oak trees.

The mountain is named for a legendary bloody battle fought by two Indian tribes, the Cherokees and the Creeks, before the white settlers arrived. The battle took place in Slaughter Gap, which lies between Blood Mountain and Slaughter Mountain, also within the wilderness.

Designated in 1991, Blood Mountain Wilderness covers 7,800 acres in the Chattahoochee National Forest. The same legislation also created the 16,400-acre Mark Trail Wilderness, a 1,160-acre addition to the Brasstown Wilderness, the 23,330-acre Ed Jenkins National Recreation Area and the 7,100-acre Coosa Bald National Scenic Area.

Blood Mountain lies west of, and across U.S. 19-129 from, Raven Cliffs Wilderness and directly south of the Coosa Bald Scenic Area. The Appalachian Trail spans nearly 11 miles in the wilderness.

Much of Blood Mountain was heavily logged and burned during

81

the early 1900s. Logging trams ran through the mountains. A second-growth forest now covers the wilderness, with most of the trees more than 60 years old.

The terrain, beginning at 1,600 feet at Dick's Creek, is generally rugged and steep.

A rare plant, three-toothed cinquefoil, is found within the wilderness. Three-toothed cinquefoil is only found at one other site in Georgia.

Blood Mountain lies about 15 miles north of Dahlonega and about 10 miles southeast of Blairsville.

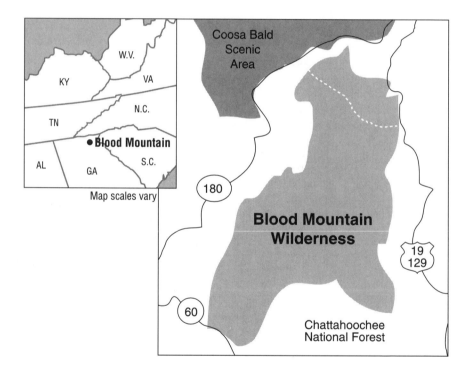

BLOOD MOUNTAIN WILDERNESS
Size: 7,800 acres.
Year designated: 1991.
Public land unit: Chattahoochee National Forest.

Features: Steep terrain; rock outcrops.
Representative wildlife: White-tailed deer; wild turkey; rainbow trout.
Wilderness map: None.
U.S.G.S. topographic maps: Coosa Bald; Neels Gap.
Counties: Lumpkin; Union.
Information: Brasstown Ranger District, P.O. Box 9, Blairsville, GA 30512. (706) 745-6928.

Brasstown Wilderness

Brasstown Wilderness nearly encircles Georgia's highest mountain, 4,784-foot Brasstown Bald and its steep ridges, remote coves and narrow valleys.

The summit of Brasstown Bald itself as well as a parking lot below the summit lie outside the wilderness in the Chattahoochee National Forest.

Thus, Brasstown Bald is a hole in a wilderness doughnut, giving visitors who drive up the mountain to the parking lot easy access to an observation tower and visitors' center on the summit.

The tower provides a panoramic view of the surrounding wilderness as well as the Chattahoochee forest and Nantahala National Forest in North Carolina.

Visitors can see into six wildernesses — Blood Mountain, Mark Trail and Raven Cliffs to the south, Tray Mountain to the southeast, Southern Nantahala to the northeast and Brasstown itself.

The name Brasstown has nothing to do with brass. It's an erroneous interpretation of the Cherokee Indian word, "Itse'yi," which means "new green place" or "place of fresh green." Several other places in the region once inhabited by the Cherokees are named "Brasstown."

The wilderness lies in northeastern Georgia just south of Chatuge Lake on the Georgia-North Carolina line, between the towns of Hiawassee and Young Harris. In 1991, the wilderness added the Rocky Knob area south of Brasstown Bald. The 1,160-acre addition increased Brasstown's size to 12,975 acres.

The expansion was part of a wilderness act that created the Blood Mountain and Mark Trail wildernesses, the Ed Jenkins National Recreation Area and the Coosa Bald National Scenic Area.

Looking out from the slopes of Brasstown, the vistas sweep across pastoral valleys reminiscent of the Shenandoah Valley in Virginia. Occasionally, the muffled sounds of civilization can be heard by visitors amid the twittering of birds and rustling of leaves.

Elevations range from 4,296 feet on Chimney Top mountain to about 2,000 feet. This range of elevation and its proximity in the Southern Appalachians means Brasstown has habitats that support northern plants and wildlife close to the southern limits of their range.

One is the New England cottontail rabbit. Another is the pygmy shrew. Ravens, which prefer high mountains, frequent the wilderness.

Brasstown's moist slopes and drier ridges have an extremely rich assortment of plants, a number of which Georgia classifies as endangered or sensitive.

These include goldenseal, ranked as endangered, fire cherry, pale

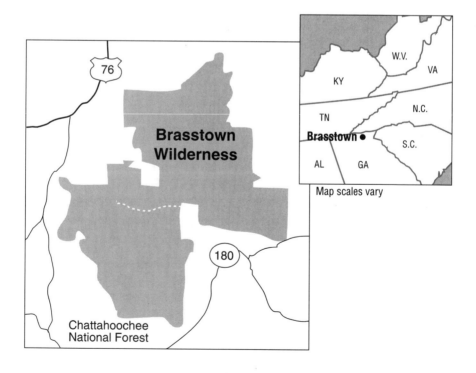

carydalis, mountain maple, blue-bead lily, kidney-leafed tway blade, mountain ash, and American false hellebore, all deemed sensitive.

More common wildflowers such as trailing arbutis, bloodroot, bluets and partridge berry can be found among the lush rhododendron and mountain laurel thickets.

The second-growth forest, a mixture of cove and uplands hardwoods, shows gradual recovery from logging of the early 20th Century. Most of the trees are older than 60 years, making Brasstown ideal for black bears and other species that require older trees for food and den sites.

Three trails totalling nearly 10 miles cut through the wilderness. Brasstown lies about 10 miles east of Blairsville.

BRASSTOWN WILDERNESS
Size: 12,975 acres.
Years designated: 1986, 1991.
Public land unit: Chattahoochee National Forest.
Features: Steep ridges and peaks; panoramic views.
Representative wildlife: White-tailed deer, wild turkey, black bear.
Wilderness map: None.
U.S.G.S. topographic maps: Hiawassee; Jack's Gap. **Counties:** Towns; Union.
Information: Brasstown Ranger District, P.O. Box 9, Blairsville, GA 30512. (706) 745-6928.

Cohutta Wilderness

Cohutta spills across 36,977 mountainous acres in northern Georgia and southeastern Tennessee, the largest national forest wilderness in the Southern Appalachians.

Congress in 1975 designated 34,102 acres of the Chattahoochee National Forest as wilderness, expanding Cohutta's northeastern boundary in 1986. All but 1,709 acres are in Georgia.

Cohutta teams up with the adjacent Big Frog Wilderness in Tennessee to form a 45,000-acre roadless block of mountains, valleys and streams.

Growing wilder by the hour, Cohutta showcases how nature can recreate a wilderness in the wake of massive logging and wildfires.

Evening primrose seeks light in Cohutta Wilderness.

No tracts of virgin forest remain. A second-growth forest of oaks and pines covers the area. The trees are nearly 75 years old. A state-maintained gravel road once entered the area but the state abandoned it in 1987. The road is now East Cowpen Trail.

Intensive logging began in 1919 in Cohutta. To ferry out the logs, timber companies built railroads along the Conasauga River and Jack's River. One wooden trestle on the Conasauga River at Rough Creek was 120 feet high. Bunk cars were winched up the hillsides and creeks for three and a half miles. Logging camps housed from 80 to 100 men.

The logging era ended in 1937. The railroads were taken apart and the rails removed. The railroad beds are still visible.

Jacks River spills through rock gorge in Cohutta Wilderness.

Like other parts of the Southern Appalachians, fires and floods struck the mountains after they had been shorn of their protective canopy of trees.

After 1937, the Forest Service purchased much of the land that makes up the wilderness for as little as $2 or $3 an acre.

Today, Cohutta imparts a sense of isolation with its spectacular gorges, swift rivers and roller-coaster terrain. It draws more hikers, hunters and fishermen than any other Southern Appalachian national forest wilderness.

The wilderness falls within the 90,000-acre Cohutta Wildlife Management Area. Black bears and wild hogs headline the wildlife here. Bears have repopulated Cohutta as they have much of the Georgia mountains in recent years. The adjoining Big Frog Wilderness in Tennessee is a bear sanctuary. While the hogs are normally nocturnal, hikers can occasionally glimpse them rooting in the forests during daylight hours.

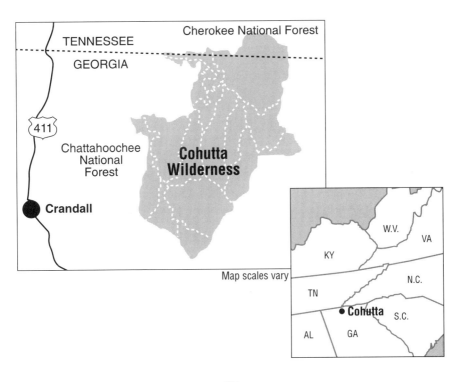

Birds are abundant. More than 100 species can be seen in Cohutta, including broad-winged hawks, great horned owls, pileated wood-peckers and a variety of warblers. Birds such as dark-eyed juncos and black-throated blue warblers that nest in northern states nest in Cohutta because of its cool climate.

Sixteen trails totalling 91 miles criss-cross Cohutta. Hikers can enter the trail network from 11 parking areas bordering the wilderness.

Cohutta lies about 10 miles east of U.S. 411 and about 20 miles north of Ellijay.

COHUTTA WILDERNESS
Size: 36,977 acres.
Years designated: 1975, 1986.
Public land units: Chattahoochee National Forest; Cherokee National Forest.
Features: Cascading waterfalls, steep gorges, more than 40 varieties of rare plants.
Representative wildlife: Black bear; wild hog; beaver.
Wilderness map: The 1:31,680-scale Cohutta and Big Frog Wilderness map.
U.S.G.S. topographic maps: Dyer Gap; Epworth; Hemp Top (Ga.); Caney Creek (Tenn).
Counties: Fannin, Gilmer and Murray counties, Ga.; Polk County, Tenn.
Information: Cohutta Ranger District, Chattahoochee National Forest, 401 Old Ellijay Road, Chatsworth, GA 30705. (706) 695-6737. Ocoee Ranger District, Cherokee National Forest, Benton, TN. (423) 338-5201.

Ellicott Rock Wilderness

See South Carolina section for a description of Ellicott Rock Wilderness.

Mark Trail Wilderness

The only wilderness named for a comic strip character, Mark Trail achieved wilderness designation in 1991 along with its neighbor to the south, Blood Mountain.

The character Mark Trail is an ardent outdoorsman who conveys a pro-conservation message in his daily adventures in the nation's newspapers. The strip was created in 1946 by Ed Dodd of nearby

Hikers leave an Appalachian Trail shelter in Mark Trail Wilderness.

Gainesville. Dodd died in 1991; Jack Elrod now draws the strip.

The second-largest mountain wilderness in Georgia after Cohutta, Mark Trail protects 16,400 acres that make up the headwater streams of the Chattahoochee River. The river supplies drinking water for Atlanta and other cities.

Once the hunting grounds of the Cherokee Indians, Mark Trail was first exploited for its gold deposits and later its timber stands.

Gold was found in Duke's Creek in 1828, immediately south of the wilderness area. Miners worked the area for years, excavating the mountain slopes for gold ore. The mining activity fell off toward the end of the 1800s as the deposits played out.

Lumber companies logged the north Georgia mountains heavily in the early 1900s, stripping Mark Trail and other parts of the Chattahoochee National Forest of its trees. At nearby Helen, one of the largest lumber mills in the East operated until about 1930.

89

A second-growth hardwood forest now covers Mark Trail, with trees now approaching 70 years old. About 14 percent of the forest consists of cove hardwoods.

Elevation ranges from 1,600 to 4,050 feet on Horsetrough Mountain. Sixteen peaks rise more than 3,500 feet. Rock outcrops and waterfalls accent the rugged scenery. Wildlife, ranging from black bear to wild turkey abound. Bear numbers are high because Mark Trail provides high-quality habitat.

On the forest floor, hikers will find plants such as golden seal, mountain maple and Goldie's wood fern.

About 15 miles of the Appalachian Trail cross Mark Trail. In addition, another five miles of trails run through the wilderness.

Mark Trail lies in about two miles northwest of Helen and about 10 miles southeast of Blairsville.

MARK TRAIL WILDERNESS
Size: 16,400 acres.

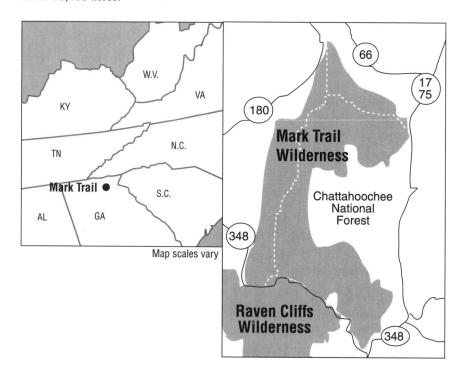

Year designated: 1991.
Public land unit: Chattahoochee National Forest.
Features: Panoramic vistas; waterfalls.
Representative wildlife: Black bear; white-tailed deer; rainbow trout.
Wilderness map: None.
U.S.G.S. topographic maps: Cowrock; Helen; Jacks Gap.
Counties: Towns; Union; White.
Information: Chattooga Ranger District, P.O. Box 196, Clarkesville, GA 30523.
(706) 754-6221.

Raven Cliffs Wilderness

A tumbling, limpid mountain stream flowing from a grotto formed by soaring cliff walls gives Raven Cliffs Wilderness a distinctive beauty.

Its 9,115 acres lie in the heart of the Chattahoochee National Forest, bounded on the north by the Mark Trail Wilderness and, on the west, across U.S. 19-129, by Blood Mountain Wilderness.

The Appalachian Trail runs along the crest of Raven Cliffs, from Neels Gap on the west to Hogpen Gap on the east, a total of 6.6 miles. The trail gives hikers vistas from rock outcrops along Wildcat Mountain and Cowrock.

The rock cliffs form habitat for birds and animals, including the raven, a high mountain bird. Black bear den in the area.

The wilderness, designated in 1986, was built around the Raven Cliffs Scenic Area, 1,600 acres that took in most of the drainage of Dodd Creek. Dodd Creek tumbles out of the rock formations, emerging at a grotto at the end of a 2.5-mile-long trail.

The Dodd Creek trail begins at state road 348, the Richard Russell Highway. The trail follows Dodd Creek and its display of chutes, cascades and pools. The two-hour hike passes by a spectacular waterfall before ending at the grotto.

The 100-foot-high rock cliffs, thick with rhododendron and hemlocks, loom over the grotto.

The area is popular with day hikers and picnickers and may be crowded during warm-weather weekends.

Raven Cliffs' mountains aren't high by Southern Appalachian

Trickle of water spills out of grotto in Raven Cliffs Wilderness.

standards; the elevation ranges from 1,800 feet to 3,846 feet on top of Levelland Mountain.

The last major logging took place between 1905 and 1920. Today, the forest is a mixture of second-growth upland and cove hardwoods and pines. Most of the trees are more than 60 years old, mature enough to provide nuts and acorns for food and cavity nests for wildlife.

As a measure of the distribution of plants and animals, the Forest Service says Raven Cliffs has an unusually high community diversity index of 1.74. The index for the Chattahoochee forest overall is 1.01.

Along with bear are white-tailed deer, grouse, turkey, raccoon and squirrel. About 36 miles of 41 miles of trout streams support native brook trout. Non-native rainbow and brown trout reproduce in the streams. Trout are stocked in the other five miles.

Forest Service surveys in valleys adjacent to Raven Cliffs have

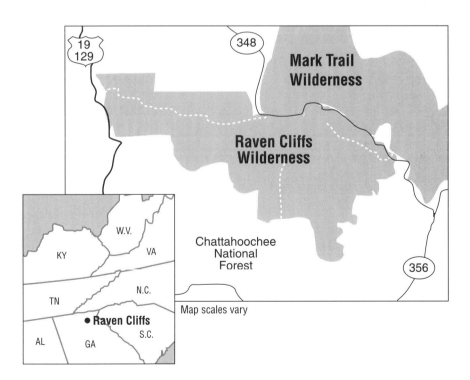

found prehistoric camp sites dating to 6000 B.C. as well as more modern remnants of log cabins, railroad beds and moonshine stills.

Raven Cliffs is about 30 miles northeast of Dahlonega and about seven miles west of Helen.

RAVEN CLIFFS WILDERNESS
Size: 9,115 acres.
Year designated: 1986.
Public land unit: Chattahoochee National Forest.
Features: Rock outcrops, streams, waterfalls.
Representative wildlife: White-tailed deer, wild turkey, brook trout.
Wilderness map: None.
U.S.G.S. topographic maps: Cowrock; Neels Gap.
Counties: Lumpkin; Union; White.
Information: Chattooga Ranger District, P.O. Box 196, Clarkesville, GA 30523. (706) 754-6221.

Rich Mountain Wilderness

Georgia's least accessible wilderness, Rich Mountain likely will remain a place that few people other than local hunters will ever visit.

It can be reached only by way of a narrow, often rutted Forest Service road. It has no scenic vistas, no protruding promontories, no maintained trails.

Rich Mountain consists of a maturing mountain forest intermingled with rushing streams and rock outcrops and criss-crossed with old logging roads.

The Forest Service described the values of Rich Mountain this way: "This wilderness is characterized as being one more of a biologic preserve than as any other single use entity such as a prime recreation area."

Consequently, Rich Mountain will receive less use and its surroundings will remain less altered by human presence than other wildernesses in Georgia.

Rich Mountain is in north-central Georgia, lying east of the towns of Blue Ridge and Ellijay. Designated in 1986, it takes in 9,649 acres of the Chattahoochee National Forest. Rich Mountain itself, a 4,050-foot-high peak, is the highest mountain in the wilderness.

Rich Mountain's forests consist of a second-growth hardwood forest between 60 and 80 years old. Only seven percent of the trees are less than 40 years old, an unusually low percentage in the heavily logged mountains of Georgia. No old-growth stands of trees exist, however.

The Rich Mountain area was settled in the period from 1830 through 1890. Settlements died out after the turn of the century when the entire area was logged in stages through 1930.

White-tailed deer, turkey and grouse are the most abundant animals. Black bear, wild hogs and woodcock also live here.

Botanically, Rich Mountain lives up to its name. It is considered to have a significant number of rare or unusual plants. Three plants found on the forest floor are classified by the state as threatened or endangered: pink lady's slipper, yellow lady's slipper and *Trientalis*

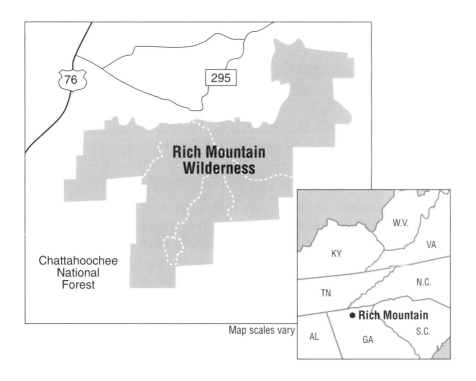

95

borealis. Other significant plants are silverbell, starflower and Goldie's fern.

RICH MOUNTAIN WILDERNESS
Size: 9,649 acres.
Year designated: 1986.
Public land unit: Chattahoochee National Forest.
Features: Maturing hardwood forest.
Representative wildlife: White-tailed deer; wild hog; black bear.
Wilderness map: None.
U.S.G.S. topographic maps: Blue Ridge; Cashes Valley; Ellijay; Tickanetley.
County: Gilmer.
Information: Toccoa Ranger District, 990 E. Main St., Suite 1, Blue Ridge, GA 30513. (706) 632-3031.

Southern Nantahala Wilderness

See North Carolina section for a description of Southern Nantahala Wilderness.

Tray Mountain Wilderness

Steep and rugged, Tray Mountain forms part of the crest of the Blue Ridge in the north Georgia mountains.

The Appalachian Trail runs 6.4 miles through the wilderness, giving hikers both solitude and a grandstand seat for scenic vistas into the surrounding Chattahoochee National Forest.

The most prominent feature in the wilderness is its namesake, 4,430-foot-high Tray Mountain. The mountain itself forms the southwestern entrance to the wilderness on the Appalachian Trail.

The wilderness, covering 9,702 acres, spreads along both the eastern and western slopes of the trail. The trail passes through the Blue Ridge Swag, a depressed, flat area along the ridge top.

The Tray Mountain area was logged heavily in the 1920s and 1930s before it became part of the national forest. A devastating forest fire swept through the area in 1952. Wilderness designation came in 1986.

The second-growth forest, now more than 60 years old, consists of oaks, yellow poplar and pitch pines. Most of the trees, about 60 percent, are chestnut, white and scarlet oaks. Some old-growth oaks that escaped the loggers' saws can be found along the ridge tops.

The maturing forest holds a few black bears along with deer, grouse and wild turkey. In spring, the forest floor comes alive with wildflowers such as violets, wild iris and toad shade (red trillium).

Among the rarer plants in Tray Mountain are golden seal, listed as endangered by the state; yellow lady slipper, listed as threatened; and red elderberry, mountain maple and rosy twisted stalk, all listed as sensitive species.

Tray Mountain lies about 10 miles northeast of Helen and about 20 miles southwest of Clayton.

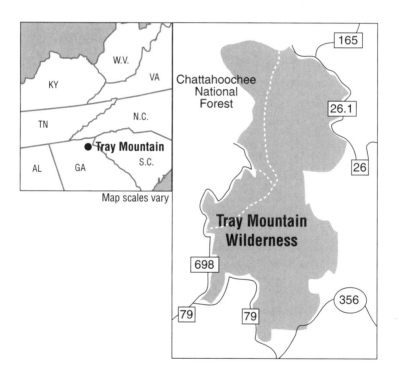

TRAY MOUNTAIN WILDERNESS
Size: 9,702 acres.
Year designated: 1986.
Public land unit: Chattahoochee National Forest.
Features: Steep, rugged terrain with panoramic vistas.
Representative wildlife: White-tailed deer, wild turkey, gray squirrel.
Wilderness map: None.
U.S.G.S. topographic map: Tray Mountain.
Counties: Towns; White.
Information: Chattooga Ranger District, P.O. Box 196, Clarkesville, GA 30523. (706) 754-6221.

Uncle Henry was asked about panthers. 'Painters?' he queried with interest. 'They is a few as uses about here. They's one, I heered, uses in Marks' Cove now. One of the Jack Creek hunters seed his hinderparts goin' through the laurel t' other day. Dogs won't hunt none thar. Thet painter's the reason, I reckon. They'll all turn tail.'

—An early 20th Century mountaineer on the Tennessee side of the Smoky Mountains, from *The Lure of the Great Smokies*, by Robert L. Mason, Houghton Mifflin Co., New York, 1927.

KENTUCKY

Beaver Creek Wilderness

Huge rock cliffs that overhang a maturing hardwood forest give Beaver Creek a sense of remoteness in the Daniel Boone National Forest.

The vertical sandstone cliffs, part of the Cumberland Plateau, were once used by Indians as shelters.

The cliffs form a 60- to 70-mile boundary that almost completely surrounds this 4,791-acre wilderness.

The wilderness resembles the fingers on a hand, following the Beaver Creek basin and the creeks that drain into it. Beaver Creek eventually flows into the Cumberland River.

A legacy of colorful names describe the wilderness's natural features. Baby Stocking Ridge and Big Swag Ridge border the wilderness while Little Hurricane Creek flows into it.

Since its acquisition by the Forest Service in the 1930s, Beaver Creek has remained relatively undisturbed. It contains old logging roads, several abandoned coal mines and former homesteads. Some old-growth trees still remain in the steep-sided hollows and less accessible areas. The area received wilderness designation in 1975.

Beaver Creek's hollows and coves hold lush stands of trees and plants. Hemlocks, ferns, mountain laurel and rhododendron form dense thickets while scarlet oak, black oak and Virginia pine live in the drier sites.

Galax, trilliums, true wood-sorrel and rue anemone are among the wildflowers that carpet the forest floor.

Beaver Creek lies within a state wildlife management area, which covers 17,347 acres in McCreary and Pulaski counties.

Deer were reintroduced in the 1950s. Squirrel, fox, raccoon, grouse and rabbit are common.

Trout stocked by the state live in the creeks but don't reproduce. The creeks, combined with the natural acidity of the water, become acidic from drainage from abandoned coal mines in and out of the wilderness.

The streams may never recover to a pristine condition. The Forest Service's roadless evaluation for Beaver Creek predicted that if stream acidity were to increase from any new acid drainage, iron concentrations would probably become toxic to fish and other aquatic life.

Beaver Creek has eight trails, totalling 18 miles.

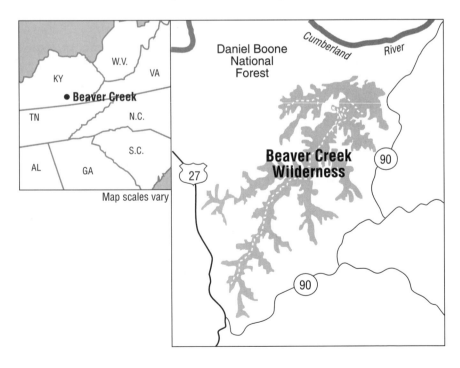

102

The wilderness is in southeastern Kentucky, about 15 miles north of Whitley City and about 10 miles northeast of Cumberland Falls State Park.

BEAVER CREEK WILDERNESS
Size: 4,791 acres.
Year designated: 1975.
Public land unit: Daniel Boone National Forest.
Features: Huge rock cliffs overlooking a maturing forest.
Representative wildlife: White-tailed deer, fox, rabbit.
Wilderness map: The 1:24,000-scale Clifty Wilderness and Beaver Creek Wilderness map.
U.S.G.S. topographic maps: Hail; Wiborg.
County: McCreary.
Information: Somerset Ranger District, 156 Realty Lane, Somerset, KY 42501. (606) 679-2010.

Clifty Wilderness

With its bridge-like arches, rugged cliffs and sinuous gorge, Clifty

Visitors view Clifty Wilderness through a massive sandstone arch.

Wilderness resembles an Eastern version of a miniature Grand Canyon.

The 12,646-acre wilderness is aptly named. The area is made up of rocky cliffs and pinnacles, carved from the scouring action of wind and water on soft sandstone rock.

Some of the spine-like cliffs jut more than 200 feet above the valley floor, giving a visitor a sense of suspension high above the wooded gorge below. Clifty attracts rock climbers, who scale and rappel the craggy palisades, as well as hikers.

Cutting through the valley floor is the Red River and its tributaries. Locally, the Clifty area is better known as the Red River Gorge, a larger area that was set aside in 1974 to protect the spectacular geologic area.

Clifty is part of the Cumberland Plateau landscape, which stretches from Ohio and West Virginia through Kentucky and south to Tennessee.

The wilderness contains a large number of prehistoric sites. Rockhouses naturally carved out of the rock were used as shelters by Native Americans for thousands of years. Archaeologists have documented the presence of people living in the gorge as far back as 8000 B.C.

The area remained untouched except by settlers until the late 1800s and early 1900s, when loggers arrived to exploit its timber.

The Kentucky Union Land Co. cut over most of the area and floated the logs down the Red River to what is now Clay City, just west of the wilderness.

The remaining settlers cultivated the portions of the broad ridge tops until 1933 when the federal government began buying tracts for the Daniel Boone National Forest.

As the forest grew back, the loggers returned. In the 1960s, mature trees in parts of Clifty fell to the ax. The biggest threat to Clifty, however, came not in the form of a saw but in that of a dam.

The U.S. Army Corps of Engineers had proposed a dam on the Red River to stop the seasonal flooding that caused damage in the downstream floodplain around Clay City.

Protesters, including the late U.S. Supreme Court Justice William Douglas, marched into the Red River Gorge in 1967 to voice their opposition to the dam that would have flooded much of what is now wilderness. The protesters won and the dam was never built.

The dam protest helped focus attention on the unique features of the gorge. In 1974 and 1975, the area was designated as the Red River Gorge Geological Area, a National Natural Landmark. Clifty was designated a wilderness in 1985.

Other parts of the Clifty ecosystem have received a measure of protection. In 1993, Congress designated 19.4 miles of the Red River as a National Wild and Scenic River, including the 4.5 miles that flow through Clifty.

More than 12 miles of trails thread by dozens of rock formations and along stream bottoms. Sheltowee Trace National Recreation Trail, a 268-mile-long footpath, passes through the northern part.

Clifty contains a mixed mesophytic forest, which dominates the Cumberland Plateau. In the Clifty area, this mixed deciduous forest

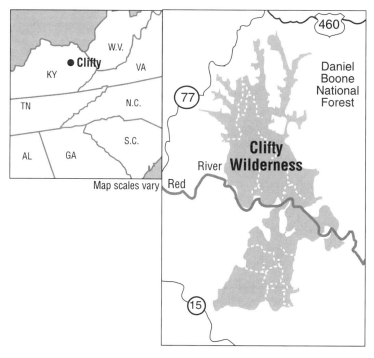

grew uninterrupted for millions of years.

The mixed mesophytic forest develops on moist, well-drained sites with a deep soil. Rather than other, simpler forest types (beech-maple and oak-hickory, for example) the mixed mesophytic forest contains about 20 or 25 species of trees. They include yellow poplar, sugar maple, beech, basswood, red oak, white oak, shagbark hickory, and, formerly, the American chestnut.

Logging altered the composition of the forest but old-growth sections of forest remain in the coves.

Clifty may have as many as 750 species of flowering plants, including 170 mosses, and 2,000 to 3,000 fungi. A unique plant species, the white-haired goldenrod, is endemic to the Red River Gorge.

Clifty is in east-central Kentucky, about 50 miles southeast of Lexington and about 10 miles northeast of Natural Bridge State Park.

CLIFTY WILDERNESS
Size: 12,646 acres.
Year designated: 1985.
Public land unit: Daniel Boone National Forest.
Features: Rock arches, pinnacles, sheer cliffs.
Representative wildlife: White-tailed deer, wild turkey, grouse.
Wilderness map: The 1:24,000-scale Clifty Wilderness and Beaver Creek Wilderness map.
U.S.G.S. topographic maps: Pomeroyton; Scranton.
Counties: Menifee; Powell; Wolfe.
Information: Stanton Ranger District, 705 W. College Ave., Stanton, KY 40380. (606) 663-2852.

Cumberland Gap National Historical Park Proposed Wilderness

Pioneers followed a path made by migrating bison through Cumberland Gap on their way to Kentucky in the late 18th and early 19th centuries.

It was America's most famous frontiersman, Daniel Boone, who scouted and marked what became known as the "Wilderness Trail" in 1775.

Cumberland Gap National Historical Park, established in 1955, commemorates this mass movement of settlers. The park covers 20,274 acres where Kentucky, Tennessee and Virginia meet. It's an area that was once called the "Roughs" of Virginia.

Within the elongated park is a proposed wilderness area of 6,375 acres and another 1,900 acres of potential wilderness.

The proposed wilderness runs from 1/4 to 1/8 mile inside the park boundaries, covering the slopes and ridges of Cumberland and Brush mountains. It stretches from The Pinnacle area on the southwest end of the park to the "White Rocks" formation at the northeast end.

Park managers recommended wilderness in 1972. In 1977, a revised recommendation of 6,375 acres of wilderness and 3,810 acres of potential wilderness was introduced in Congress. Then, a year later, another revision calling for 12,191 acres of wilderness and 1,900 acres of potential wilderness was incorporated into an appropriation

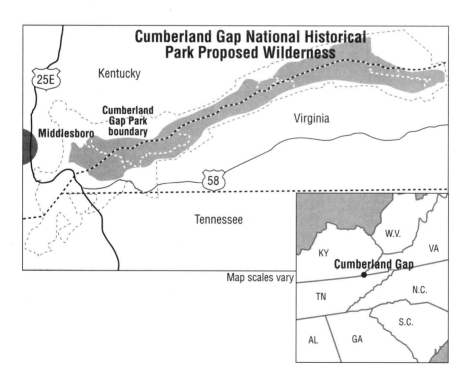

107

bill for the National Park Service.

The revised wilderness proposal was dropped on objections from Virginia officials who were interested in developing the area of the park that runs along the Virginia side. Most of the proposed wilderness lies on the Virginia side.

Congress has taken no further action and the wilderness proposal languishes.

The park's 1978 master plan calls for 6,375 acres of wilderness and 1,900 acres of potential wilderness. Park officials continue to manage the area for its natural values. They have banned wheeled vehicles in the "backcountry," as they call the area, and require permits for overnight camping. The park closes at night.

Most of the park's main trail, the 19-mile-long Ridge Trail, falls within the proposed wilderness. Hikers can pick up the trail at The Pinnacle. At its widest part, the proposed wilderness conveys a sense of solitude. Even in winter, with the trees shorn of their leaves, only a house or two can be seen in the distance. The intrusive sounds of traffic on U.S. 25E mostly disappeared in 1996 with the opening of Cumberland Gap Tunnel.

The rolling Ridge Trail passes through a hickory-oak forest mixed with Virginia, shortleaf and pitch pines, rhododendron and mountain laurel. Wildflowers, such as trailing arbutus, are abundant in spring. Hikers may see white-tailed deer, raccoons, red squirrels and songbirds. Black bear have recently migrated into the park.

The trail passes by limestone caves and Goose Nest, a spectacular sinkhole (a vertical cave) and numerous rock outcrops.

At the eastern end of the park is the "White Rocks," a massive rock formation that pioneers heading for Cumberland Gap used as a landmark signifying they were nearing the gap. Elevations in this area reach 3,500 feet, highest in the park. The park has 55 miles of trails.

CUMBERLAND GAP NATIONAL HISTORICAL PARK
Size: 6,375 acres proposed (an additional 1,900 acres is potential wilderness).
Year designated: Not designated.

Public land unit: Cumberland Gap National Historical Park.

Features: Rock outcroppings; limestone caves; rolling ridges.

Representative wildlife: White-tailed deer; raccoon; pileated woodpecker.

Wilderness map: None.

U.S.G.S. topographic maps: Ewing; Middlesboro North and South; Varilla; Wheeler.

Counties: Bell County, Ky.; Claiborne County, Tenn.; and Lee County, Va.

Information: Cumberland Gap National Historical Park, P.O. Box 1848, Middlesboro, Ky. 40965. (606) 248-2817.

This is the beginning of the Smoky Mountain chain proper, which by the general elevation both of its peaks and its crest, by its perfect continuity, its great roughness and difficulty of approach, may be called the master chain of the Appalachian system...Between the gorges of the Big Pigeon and Road Gap the top of these ridges is usually sharp and rocky, deeply indented, and winding considerably, covered with a dense growth of Laurel and high trees, which make travel over them extremely difficult and almost impracticable. Neither the White man nor the Indian hunter venture in this wilderness.

—Geographer Arnold Guyot, describing the Great Smoky Mountains in his 1856-60 survey of the Southern Appalachians, as quoted is the *North Carolina Historical Review* in July, 1938.

NORTH CAROLINA

Craggy Mountain Wilderness Study Area

Craggy Mountain ties a mile-high section of the Blue Ridge Parkway to a sloping hardwood cove forest in the Pisgah National Forest.

The parkway forms the southern boundary of Craggy Mountain's 2,380 acres. Craggy Mountain descends from 5,600 feet to 3,000 feet into a valley formed by Carter Creek.

The wilderness study area begins just east of the Craggy Gardens visitors' center on the parkway.

Craggy Mountain's forest consists of cove and upland hardwoods with an understory of rhododendron, mountain laurel and blueberry.

The lower elevations have been logged. Most of the trees are from 60 to 80 years old, mixed with old-growth stands of hemlock and yellow birch on the upper slopes.

More than a dozen rare species of plants, including spreading avens, one-flowered rush and Gray's lily, live in the study area.

A 950-acre core of Craggy Mountain had been protected since 1961 as a scenic area. Congress designated Craggy Mountain a wilderness study area in the 1984 North Carolina Wilderness Act. The Forest Service recommended wilderness for Craggy Mountain in 1987.

But Craggy Mountain's future has been tied to two other study areas, Overflow and Snowbird.

Turks cap lily unfurls flower in Craggy Mountain Wilderness Study Area.

All three lie in the 11th Congressional District of Rep. Charles Taylor, R-N.C. He favors wilderness for Craggy Mountain but opposes designation for Overflow and Snowbird in the Nantahala National Forest.

Opposition from U.S. Sen. Jesse Helms, R-N.C., further complicates Craggy Mountain's future. In 1993, Helms proposed a swap. He indicated he'd support wilderness designation for two other Pisgah National Forest wilderness study areas, Harper Creek and Lost Cove. His support was conditioned on the release of Overflow and Snowbird for general use, including logging.

Wilderness advocates, however, spurned the compromise. Thus, Craggy Mountain and the others remain wilderness study areas until the stalemate is resolved. The Forest Service continues to manage all five to protect their wilderness values.

Craggy Mountain has two trails totalling about three miles. It's 20 miles northeast of Asheville and about five miles south of Mount Mitchell, at 6,684 feet the highest peak in the East.

CRAGGY MOUNTAIN WILDERNESS STUDY AREA
Size: 2,380 acres.
Year designated: Not designated.
Public land unit: Pisgah National Forest.
Features: Cove hardwoods; rare plants.
Representative wildlife: Black bear; wild turkey; red squirrel.
Wilderness map: None.
U.S.G.S. topographic maps: Craggy Pinnacle; Montreat.

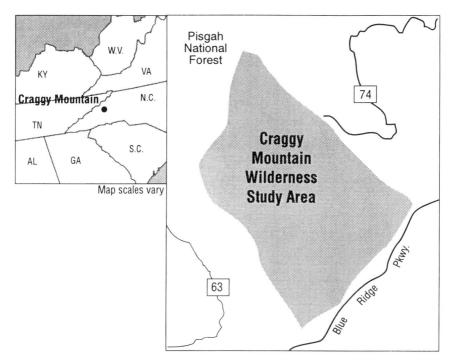

County: Buncombe.
Information: Toecane Ranger District, Box 128, Burnsville, NC 28714. (704) 682-6146.

Ellicott Rock Wilderness

See South Carolina section for a description of Ellicott Rock Wilderness.

Great Smoky Mountains National Park Proposed Wilderness

Black bears and red wolves. More than 100,000 acres of old-growth forest. The greatest variety of salamanders — 27 — of any comparably-sized area in the world.

These are some of the superlatives that define Great Smoky Mountains National Park, which has the largest remaining tract of original Southern Appalachian wilderness.

115

The park covers 520,409 acres in North Carolina and Tennessee. Most of the park, 53 percent, falls on the North Carolina side. About three-fifths of the park's boundary joins three national forests, the Cherokee in Tennessee and the Nantahala and Pisgah in North Carolina. Thus, the park forms the core of a much larger ecosystem.

The Smokies also claim:

• Sixteen peaks higher than 6,000 feet, including Clingman's Dome, at 6,643 feet the highest peak in Tennessee.

• One hundred species of trees, more than all of northern Europe, and 1,275 species of flowering plants.

• Sixty species of mammals and 238 species of songbirds.

• The two largest roadless areas in the Southern Appalachians. At Tri-Corner Knob, the distance to the nearest road is 8.8 miles. This is one of the greatest distances one can walk in a direct route in any direction in the Southern Appalachians before hitting a road.

The National Park Service in 1982 recommended wilderness for as many as 466,000 acres and has been managing the area as wilderness ever since. But a political dispute over a proposed road has blocked designation by Congress.

Great Smokies can trace its origin to the early 1900s. Horace Kephart, a St. Louis librarian who moved to the Smokies in 1904, wrote books and articles that urged a park in the Smokies. In the early 1920s, Knoxville, Tenn., and Asheville, N.C., residents organized to promote a park as loggers cut into the high peaks.

Great Smoky Mountains National Park

Black-chinned red salamander thrives in Great Smoky Mountains National Park Proposed Wilderness.

The dream became a reality in 1926 when Congress passed enabling legislation. The original legislation called for a park of 704,000 acres; the size eventually

116

shrank to 468,000 acres.

Each state donated $2 million for land acquisition while civic groups, private individuals and school kids came up with thousands of dollars. Oil magnate John Rockefeller Jr. donated $5 million and Congress put up the rest of the money. The park opened in 1934.

Nine years later, the park expanded to its present size when the Tennessee Valley Authority bought land in Swain County, N.C., to create Fontana Lake. The utility gave the park 44,000 acres.

Filling the lake flooded 14 communities and a state road, cutting off access to family cemeteries. The Department of Interior agreed to build a new road to the cemeteries along the north shore of the lake. The promise was contingent on Congress appropriating the money after World War II.

But conservationists objected to the 30-mile road west of Bryson City in Swain County. The park service paved 2.5 miles in the early 1960s, then halted work.

The proposed road remains at the center of a stalemate over wilderness designation. Since 1987, proponents in both states have pushed a wilderness bill.

The legislation has been blocked by Sen. Jesse Helms, R- N.C. Helms has allied himself with a group of Swain County residents who want the federal government to build the road so they can drive to family cemeteries in the park. Park officials now shuttle them by boat.

Helms has supported a smaller, 422,000-acre wilderness proposal that excludes the area for the road. In turn, park officials and wilderness proponents back a settlement that would pay Swain County $16 million to compensate for the road. Swain officials have rejected the settlement. In 1995, Helms introduced a bill calling for both the $16-million payment to Swain County and completion of the road. The issue remains unresolved.

The nation's most-visited national park draws about nine million people a year. Visitors marvel at the park's cloud-swathed peaks, cascading waterfalls and maturing forests.

An old-growth forest of more than 100,000 acres lies mostly on the Tennessee side. These old-growth areas include the Albright Grove area with tulip-poplar and Eastern hemlock. Albright Grove has a 265-year-old hemlock whose trunk diameter measures eight feet, four inches. Some standing trees have been alive for as long as 500 years.

Some 400 to 600 black bears roam the park, forming a core population in the Southern Appalachians; about 100 bears disperse into surrounding lands each year.

White-tailed deer seek open meadows and edges, clustering in valleys like Cades Cove. Groundhogs, bobcats, beaver, mink and red squirrels all find their niche.

The park is the only known place in the East in which numbers of migratory songbirds, on the decline elsewhere, have remained constant, according to Dr. John Terborgh, author of *Where Have All The Birds Gone?*

Terborgh surmises the size of the park and its expanses of road-free forest keep it safe from exotic cowbirds, which lay their eggs in the nests of other birds. Baby cowbirds push the host birds' young out of the nest. Terborgh says for an area to be free from cowbirds, it must contain at least 37,000 acres of unbroken forest.

The park is a sanctuary for federally threatened and endangered species.

Once absent, 13 peregrine falcons have been released since 1984. The red wolf, the native wolf of the Southeast, was restored in 1991. About 10 adult wolves now live in the Cades Cove and Tremont areas; wolf releases are to continue.

Park officials have restored to park streams a tiny catfish called the smoky madtom, once believed extinct, and another small fish, the spotfin chub. Other endangered species are the Carolina northern flying squirrel, the Indiana bat (which roosts in two of the park's nine caves) and the red-cockaded woodpecker.

Extirpated animals have returned. Since the 1980s, park managers have released 135 otters into the creeks.

Two other animals, elk and fisher, might return as part of the park's mandate to restore native species.

Elk, hunted out in the early 1800s, could occupy the spruce-fir forest and meadows.

A 1996 survey by the University of Tennessee showed the park contained adequate habitat for more than 50 individual elk in several herds. Park officials say, however, that elk restoration isn't likely immediately because the park has no money to pay monitoring costs.

Fishers, weasel-like animals, were wiped out by the early 1900s by trappers who sought the animals' silky, dark-brown fur. The park hasn't taken steps to stock fishers proposed in a restoration plan.

Exotic species have taken over parts of the park, inflicting long-term damage.

The red spruce-Fraser fir forest has been ravaged since the 1960s by an insect pest, the balsam woolly adelgid. It has killed more than 95 percent of the mature Fraser firs. With no protective canopy, sunshine dries out the moist, moss-covered ground. The drying has eliminated an inhabitant, the spruce-fir moss spider. The federally endangered spider is a tarantula the size of a BB shot.

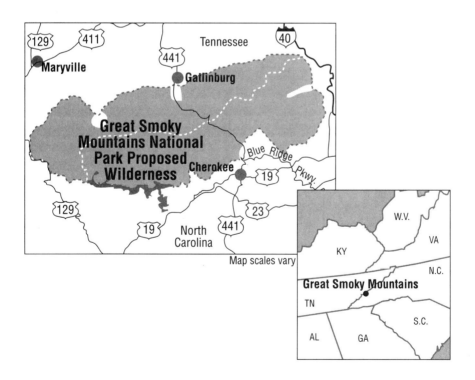

119

Wild hogs entered the park about 1940. The hogs root up the forest floor and wallow in springs. Park officials have used a combination of trapping and shooting to reduce hog numbers, which vary from several hundred to as many as 1,000 during the year.

The park views two other non-natives, brown and rainbow trout, more benignly. The trout were stocked in the early 1900s to replace native brook trout that had been eliminated by logging. The more aggressive rainbows have displaced brook trout from about 70% of the native's range.

Hikers can choose from among more than 800 miles of trails, including nearly 70 miles of the Appalachian Trail.

GREAT SMOKY MOUNTAINS NATIONAL PARK PROPOSED WILDERNESS
Size: As much as 466,000 acres.
Year designated: Not designated.
Public land unit: Great Smoky Mountains National Park.
Features: More than 100,000 acres of old-growth forest; 16 peaks above 6,000 feet.
Representative wildlife: Black bear; red wolf; salamanders.
Wilderness map: Great Smoky Mountains Trail Map.
U.S.G.S. topographic map: Great Smoky Mountains National Park.
Counties: Graham, Haywood and Swain counties, N.C.; Blount, Cocke and Sevier counties, Tenn.
Information: Great Smoky Mountains National Park, 107 Park Headquarters Road, Gatlinburg, TN 37738. (423) 436-1200.

Harper Creek Wilderness Study Area
Lost Cove Wilderness Study Area

Waterfalls, a box canyon and a forest mixed with old-growth trees highlight two wilderness study areas in the Pisgah National Forest.

Harper Creek and Lost Cove Wilderness Study Areas lie side by side on the eastern slopes of the Blue Ridge Parkway. The two study areas spread across 12,850 acres separated only by a dirt road.

Located on the Blue Ridge Escarpment, the dividing line between the mountains and the Piedmont, Harper Creek alone claims five waterfalls. One plunges 200 feet into an unusual box canyon.

Farther downstream, on Harper Creek itself, a three-tiered waterfall splashes into upper and lower pools near the eastern edge of the study area.

Dense foliage and narrow, winding valleys give the 7,140 acres in Harper Creek a sense of isolation in relatively low mountains. Elevations range from 1,600 to 4,000 feet.

Just to the north, Lost Cove's 5,710 acres have remained virtually untouched since it was swept by wildfire in 1927. The forest of oaks, hickories and pines is about 70 years old. Like Harper Creek, Lost Cove is a state black bear sanctuary.

Near the western edge of the Lost Cove study area are the Lost Cove Cliffs. These rock formations rise 1,200 feet above the forested valley below.

Harper Creek and Lost Cove were designated study areas by Congress in the North Carolina Wilderness Act of 1984. The Forest Service recommended wilderness for the two in 1987.

Lost Cove Creek plunges into pool in Lost Cove Wilderness Study Area.

In 1990, U.S. Rep. Cass Ballenger, R-N.C., introduced bills to designate Harper Creek and Lost Cove as wilderness. The bills passed the House that year but ran into opposition in the Senate. They were opposed by Sen. Jesse Helms, R-N.C.

The political stalemate over Harper Creek, Lost Cove and three other study areas is described in the Craggy Mountain Wilderness Study Area profile.

Harper Creek and Lost Cove are about 30 miles north of Morganton and about 25 miles south of Boone.

HARPER CREEK WILDERNESS STUDY AREA
Size: 7,140 acres.
Year designated: Not designated.
Public land unit: Pisgah National Forest.
Features: Waterfalls, box canyon.
Representative wildlife: Black bear; white-tailed deer.
Wilderness map: The 1:24,000-scale Wilson Creek Area Trail map.
U.S.G.S. topographic maps: Chestnut Mountain; Grandfather Mountain.

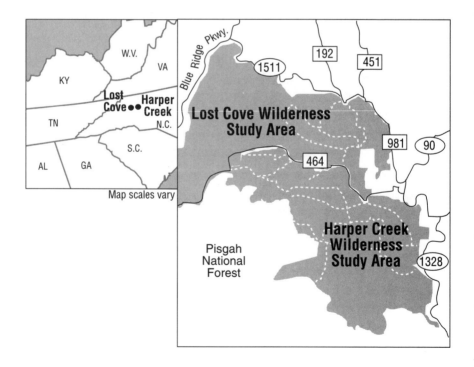

122

Counties: Avery; Caldwell.
Information: Grandfather Ranger District, Box 519, Marion, NC 28752. (704) 652-2144.

<small>LOST COVE WILDERNESS STUDY AREA</small>
Size: 5,710 acres.
Year designated: Not designated.
Public land unit: Pisgah National Forest.
Features: Steep cliffs; aging forest.
Representative wildlife: Black bear; white-tailed deer.
Wilderness map: The 1:24,000-scale Wilson Creek Area Trail map.
U.S.G.S. topographic map: Grandfather Mountain.
Counties: Avery; Caldwell.
Information: Grandfather Ranger District, Pisgah National Forest, Box 519, Marion, NC 28752. (704) 652-2144.

Joyce Kilmer-Slickrock Wilderness

Joyce Kilmer-Slickrock safeguards one of the largest enclaves of old-growth forest in the East.

The 17,394-acre wilderness holds huge tulip-poplars and Eastern hemlocks that measure more than 20 feet around at the base. Many trees are estimated to be 300 to 400 years old.

In the shady coves, life teems among ferns, mosses and wildflowers. Red-cheeked salamanders burrow in the moldering logs; hooded warblers trill from their perches hidden within the 100-foot-high canopy.

Above, on the slopes of 5,249-foot-high Haoe mountain, the second-highest point in the wilderness, black bears and wild hogs forage for nuts. In 1996, a red wolf wandered in from Great Smoky Mountains National Park to make his home here.

The Joyce Kilmer section covers nearly 3,800 acres of old-growth cove hardwood and upland hardwood forest in the Little Santeetlah Creek watershed. The Slickrock section lies across an east-west ridge that divides the wilderness. Slickrock Creek contains remnants of old-growth forest in the higher elevations.

The Unicoi Mountains mark the boundary between Joyce Kilmer-Slickrock and Citico Creek Wilderness in Tennessee. Citico

123

Creek's 16,226 acres contribute to an unbroken wilderness complex of nearly 30,000 acres.

Joyce Kilmer-Slickrock was hewn out of the far-western part of the Nantahala National Forest in North Carolina and the Cherokee National Forest in Tennessee.

In 1915, the Babcock Land and Lumber Co. began logging in the Slickrock area. The company built a railroad into the watershed, gradually extending it southward as its loggers cleared the forest.

Babcock stopped logging in 1922 and pulled out of Slickrock. A dam on the Little Tennessee River soon would form a lake that would flood the railroad line. Without the creation of Calderwood Lake, the old-growth forest would have been cut.

The Forest Service bought the Slickrock watershed from Babcock in 1935. The area had been logged and scorched by uncontrolled fires.

In that same year, at the request of the Veterans of Foreign Wars, the Forest Service also sought out an undisturbed tract to be named in honor of Joyce Kilmer, author of the poem "Trees". Kilmer was 31 when he was killed in service in World War I. The agency selected a 3,800-acre parcel of virgin timber at the western edge of Nantahala and dedicated it in memory of the young New Jersey poet.

By the 1960s, Slickrock's trees had grown back to the point that the Forest Service designated 600 acres for timber cutting. The proposal aroused the concern of two conservation groups, The Wilderness Society and Trout Unlimited. They convinced the Forest Service to study Slickrock for wilderness.

Meanwhile, another threat to Joyce Kilmer-Slickrock arose. A scenic highway was proposed in the late 1950s to link Tellico Plains, Tenn., and Robbinsville, N.C.

The route would have crossed the 5,000-foot-high ridge that separates Joyce Kilmer from Slickrock, splitting the wild area in two. The Forest Service approved construction in 1964.

The highway touched off a national controversy, leading to a wilderness study by the Forest Service. Meanwhile, the Federal Highway Administration chose another route south of Joyce

Decaying chestnut tree stands among 400-year-old trees in old-growth forest in Joyce Kilmer-Slickrock Wilderness.

Kilmer-Slickrock. The scenic Cherohala Skyway opened in 1996.

Congress designated Joyce Kilmer-Slickrock Wilderness in 1975. The 10,200-acre wilderness was expanded in 1984 to its present size.

Most people limit their visit to the Joyce Kilmer Memorial Trail, which loops through a cove forest dominated by tulip-poplars.

Overall, the wilderness has a network of 60 miles of trails.

Joyce Kilmer-Slickrock is 12

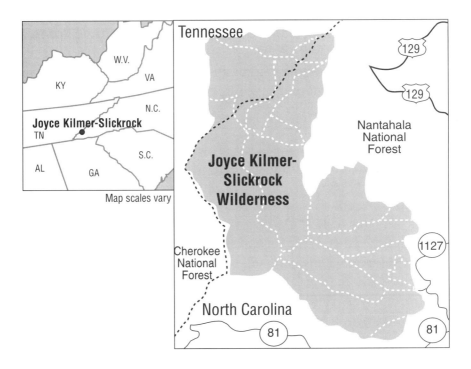

miles west of Robbinsville and about 15 miles east of Tellico Plains, in Graham County, N.C. and Monroe County, Tenn.

JOYCE KILMER-SLICKROCK WILDERNESS
Size: 17,394 acres.
Years designated: 1975, 1984.
Public land units: Nantahala National Forest; Cherokee National Forest.
Features: Old-growth forest; giant trees; remote peaks and coves.
Representative wildlife: Black bear; hooded warbler; brook trout.
Wilderness map: The 1:24,000-scale Joyce Kilmer-Slickrock Wilderness and Citico Creek Wilderness map.
U.S.G.S. topographic maps: Santeetlah Creek; Tapoco.
Counties: Graham County, N.C.; Monroe County, Tenn.
Information: Cheoah Ranger District, Route 1, Box 16-A, Robbinsville, NC 28771. (704) 479-6431.

Linville Gorge Wilderness

Linville Gorge, a 2,000-foot-deep canyon that winds through part of the Pisgah National Forest, looks more like Idaho than North Carolina.

Visitors can marvel at the gorge's rock palisades, its whitewater river and its old-growth forest.

Linville Gorge is one of the deepest canyons in the East. The Linville River flows through the serpentine, 12-mile-long gorge. The Cherokee Indians named the river Eeseeoh, which means "river of many cliffs."

The river and gorge take their present name from explorer John Linville and his son, also named John, who were killed in 1776 in the gorge by Cherokees.

Geographer Arnold Guyot visited Linville Gorge in 1856-60. Here is how he described it: "Two main ridges run from the Blue Ridge to the South, the chain of the Hawksbill and Table Rock from the Grandfather (Mountain) and the Linville chain, further west. Between these spurs the Linville river flows in a fearful and perfectly impassable chasm, into which it precipitates itself from the plateau of the Grandfather forming magnificent waterfalls."

The Forest Service has managed Linville Gorge for its wilder-

Donna Bise

Turkey beard flower brightens forest floor in Linville Gorge Wilderness.

ness values since acquisition in 1938. In 1951, the agency designated Linville Gorge as primitive area, giving it administrative protection.

Linville Gorge was one of three wildernesses created in the East in 1964 with enactment of the Wilderness Act. The other two were Shining Rock in North Carolina and Great Gulf in New Hampshire.

Congress initially set aside 7,575 acres of the upper gorge as wilderness, then expanded the wilderness area to the lower gorge in 1984. The present size is 12,002 acres.

The upper gorge begins just southeast of the Blue Ridge Parkway. Pinnacles and outcroppings of rocks form the gorge's upper wall. Among these formations is The Chimneys, a group of pinnacles on the eastern rim. Some jut into the gorge, looking like flying buttresses on medieval cathedrals.

Elevations range from 3,000 to 3,500 feet along the rims. The highest point is 4,120-foot-high Gingercake Mountain on the northeast corner. Two distinctive landmarks are Table Rock Mountain and Hawksbill, a jagged peak whose outline resembles the bill of a hawk.

The steepness of the gorge kept loggers from cutting Linville Gorge's trees. Hikers can see standing snags and decaying logs of American chestnuts in the old-growth forest.

The gorge harbors several species of endangered animals and plants.

Peregrine falcons soar over the gorge, restored in the mid-1980s by federal and state wildlife agencies. The Forest Service closes part of Linville Gorge (including the entire North Carolina Wall) for rock climbing and rapelling from January 15 through July 15 to provide solitude for nesting falcons.

Two federally endangered plants live in the gorge. One is Heller's blazing star. The other is mountain golden heather, a juniper-like plant that's only found in Linville Gorge and a few nearby places.

Located on dry ridges, mountain golden heather depends on periodic wildfire to get enough sunlight to prosper. Fire suppression brought mountain golden heather to the brink of extinction. By 1989, the number of plants had fallen to 1,500 or so, a critically low number.

Biologists started using controlled burns to clear out competing plants and shrubs, enabling seeds to sprout naturally. In 1994, the state reintroduced heather seedlings grown in a greenhouse to bolster the plant's chance for recovery.

Hikers can choose from among 17 trails totalling 22 miles. Overnight use is limited because of heavy visitation in summer. The Forest Service requires permits from May 1 through Oct. 31 for camp-

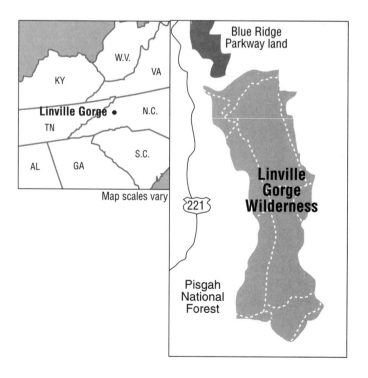

ing on weekends and holidays, with a maximum of 50 people. The permits are free. No permits are required from Nov. 1 through April 30 or anytime for day trips.

Overnight visitors can remain in the gorge for no more than three consecutive days. Groups may not exceed 10 people, a rule that applies to all wildernesses in North Carolina.

Linville Gorge is about 60 miles northeast of Asheville.

LINVILLE GORGE WILDERNESS
Size: 12,002 acres.
Years designated: 1964, 1984.
Public land unit: Pisgah National Forest.
Features: Steep, twisting gorge; old-growth forest.
Representative wildlife: Black bear; peregrine falcon; white-tailed deer.
Wilderness map: The 1:24,000-scale Linville Gorge Wilderness map.
U.S.G.S. topographic maps: Ashford; Linville Falls.
Counties: Burke; McDowell.
Information: Grandfather Ranger District, Route 1, Box 110-A, Nebo, NC 28761. (704) 652-2144.

Lost Cove Wilderness Study Area

See Harper Creek Wilderness Study Area for a description of Lost Cove Wilderness Study Area.

Middle Prong Wilderness
Shining Rock Wilderness

Peaks surpassing 6,000 feet and panoramic vistas make Middle Prong and Shining Rock two of the most popular wilderness areas in the Southern Appalachians.

The two wildernesses separated by a road cover 25,943 acres in the Pisgah National Forest. The Blue Ridge Parkway provides easy access to both.

Elevations in the two wildernesses range from 6,400 feet in the southwest corner of Middle Prong to 3,200 feet in both wildernesses. In Shining Rock, Big Sam Knob and Cold Mountain both top 6,000 feet.

129

Hikers gather to watch sunset on quartz outcrop in Shining Rock Wilderness.

Shining Rock draws its name from white quartz outcroppings on the Shining Rock peak. Campfires are banned year round in Shining Rock and Middle Prong.

A well-used network of trails criss-cross both wilderness areas. North Carolina's Mountains to the Sea Trail cuts across the southern tier of Middle Prong. The Art Loeb Trail crosses 6,214-foot-high Black Balsam Knob before entering Shining Rock from the south. It then becomes Ivestor Gap Trail on its way to Shining Rock Gap.

Lesser-known Middle Prong, drained by the west fork of the Pigeon River, offers its own stunning views from peaks like 5,880-foot-high Green Knob. Like Shining Rock, the peaks support stands of red spruce, hemlocks and a few Fraser firs. Middle Prong is a state black bear sanctuary.

North Carolina's state Natural Heritage Program lists the mature beech-buckeye forest at Mount Hardy Gap at Middle Prong's southern boundary as one of the best examples of its kind in the Southern Appalachians.

In addition, the 6,100-foot-high Mount Hardy has a mixture of red spruce and Fraser fir forest, grass and heath balds and high-elevation seeps and bogs.

The top-of-the-world beauty of the wildernesses belies the devastation that has hit both.

Logging began at the beginning of the 20th Century. Massive fires broke out in 1925 — a year of record drought — and 1942. Fires shaped the landscape, creating the grassy balds, blueberry bushes and a palette of wildflowers.

It was near here that the last wild wolf in North Carolina, and perhaps the entire Southern Appalachians, was shot in 1933. The wolf probably was a straggler, the last of its kind.

Shining Rock was one of three original wildernesses designated in the East in 1964. The others were Linville Gorge in North Carolina and Great Gulf in New Hampshire.

Shining Rock's original size of 13,600 acres was expanded to 18,533 acres in 1984. The same legislation created 7,460-acre Middle Prong Wilderness to the west. Two-lane N.C. 215 separates the two wildernesses.

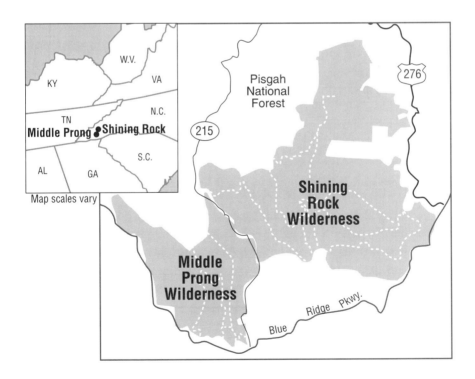

Middle Prong and Shining Rock are bounded on the south by the Blue Ridge Parkway, about 25 miles southwest of Asheville.

MIDDLE PRONG WILDERNESS
Size: 7,460 acres.
Year designated: 1984.
Public land unit: Pisgah National Forest.
Features: Grassy balds, mixed conifer-hardwood forest.
Representative wildlife: Black bear; white-tailed deer.
Wilderness map: The 1:24,000-scale Shining Rock Wilderness and Middle Prong Wilderness map.
U.S.G.S. topographic maps: Sam Knob; Waynesville.
County: Haywood.
Information: Pisgah Ranger District, 1001 Pisgah Highway, Pisgah Forest, NC 28768. (704) 877-3350.

SHINING ROCK WILDERNESS
Size: 18,483 acres.
Years designated: 1964, 1984.
Public land unit: Pisgah National Forest.
Features: Large outcrop of quartz rock; grassy and heath balds; peaks over 6,000 feet.
Representative wildlife: Black bear; white-tailed deer, hawks.
Wilderness map: The 1:24,000-scale Shining Rock Wilderness and Middle Prong Wilderness map.
U.S.G.S. topographic maps: Cruso; Sam Knob; Shining Rock.
County: Haywood.
Information: Pisgah Ranger District, 1001 Pisgah Highway, Pisgah Forest, NC 28768. (704) 877-3350.

Overflow Wilderness Study Area

Overflow fills a bowl-shaped valley in the Nantahala National Forest renowned for its stunning scenery.

The study area is named for Overflow Creek, which feeds the Chattooga River to the south and east.

Also known locally as Blue Valley, Overflow consists of 3,200 acres of pines and hardwoods in a forest that's between 60 and 80 years old.

From NC 106, a highway that borders Overflow on the north, the valley gives the appearance of an unbroken mountain forest stretching to the horizon.

Elevations in Overflow range from 2,500 to 4,100 feet. Osage Mountain looms over Overflow's western boundary, near where Overflow's main trail passes. The trail is part of the 68-mile-long Bartram Trail, established to follow the route taken by the 18th Century naturalist William Bartram of Philadelphia.

Bartram traveled through the area in the late 1700s, collecting plant specimens. In 1791, he published a book of his adventures, *Travels Through North and South Carolina, Georgia, East and West Florida.*

The Bartram Trail runs from Rabun Bald in Georgia west to Cheoah Bald in North Carolina. It is marked by yellow blazes on trees and rocks. In lush, moist Overflow, much of the trail goes through tunnels of rhododendron and crosses numerous streams over slab-log foot bridges.

Overflow became a Wilderness Study Area in 1984. Since, Overflow has been at the center of a political tug-of-war over whether it should be wilderness.

Indian pipes, a fungus-dependent plant, rise from the soil in Overflow Wilderness Study Area.

Forest officials later recommended against the area for wilderness, concluding that Overflow's small size didn't justify designation.

U.S. Rep. Charles Taylor, R-N.C., opposes designation of both Overflow and Snowbird as wilderness, favoring releasing the areas to the Forest Service for general use, including logging.

But wilderness advocates and many residents in the Highlands area next to

Overflow continue to call for protecting Overflow as wilderness. The result is a stalemate, leaving Overflow as a study area indefinitely.

Overflow lies near a 3,950-acre wild area in the Chattahoochee National Forest in Georgia called Overflow. Chattahoochee forest managers also rejected wilderness designation for the Georgia Overflow but classified it as a semi-primitive, non-motorized area.

Overflow is in Macon County, about five miles southwest of Highlands and about 25 miles southeast of Franklin in Western North Carolina.

OVERFLOW WILDERNESS STUDY AREA
Size: 3,200 acres.
Year designated: Not designated.
Public land unit: Nantahala National Forest.
Features: Bowl-like basin set among mountain ridges.
Representative wildlife: Wild turkey, white-tailed deer, grouse.
Wilderness map: None.
U.S.G.S. topographic map: Scaly Mountain.

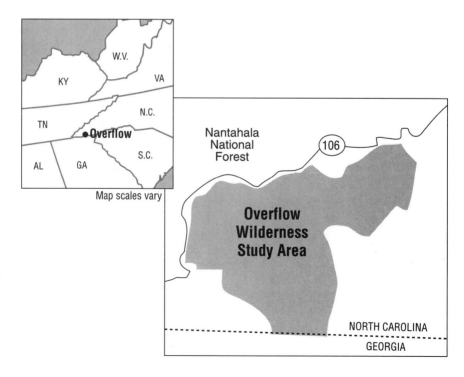

County: Macon.
Information: Highlands Ranger District, 2010 Flat Mountain Road, Highlands, NC 28741. (704) 526-3765.

Shining Rock Wilderness

See Middle Prong Wilderness for a description of Shining Rock Wilderness.

Snowbird Wilderness Study Area

Snowbird embraces 8,490 acres of the Snowbird and Unicoi mountain ranges in the Nantahala National Forest in far Western North Carolina.

Rugged and steep, elevations range from 2,600 to 5,429 feet on Hooper Bald. Remnant stands of old-growth forest populate the upper slopes; the forests on the lower slopes are 60 to 80 years old.

Snowbird harbors black bear and wild hogs. Native brook trout live above Big Falls in Snowbird Creek.

The Snowbird area was one of the last places in North Carolina to be settled. Timber companies came in the late 1800s, taking out huge tulip-poplars and chestnuts that cloaked the coves and slopes.

In 1927 Bemis Lumber Company purchased the "Big Snowbird" watershed. From 1928 to 1942, according to the Forest Service reports, loggers removed 100 million board feet of lumber by way of the Buffalo-Snowbird Railroad.

The Forest Service in 1943 bought Big Snowbird, making it part of Nantahala National Forest.

A study area since 1984, Snowbird failed to get a recommendation for wilderness designation from the Forest Service. Anti-wilderness sentiment in sparsely populated Graham County runs high due to historic hostility to federal regulations.

Snowbird and four other study areas have been tied up in a political stalemate described in the Craggy Mountain Wilderness Study Area profile. The Forest Service continues to manage Snowbird for its wilderness values. A network of seven trails lead along the ridges and the interior of the Snowbird basin to its highest points along the

Tennessee state line.

Joyce Kilmer-Slickrock Wilderness lies about 10 miles to the north while Citico Creek Wilderness in Tennessee lies about 10 miles northwest.

Snowbird is about 10 miles west of Robbinsville.

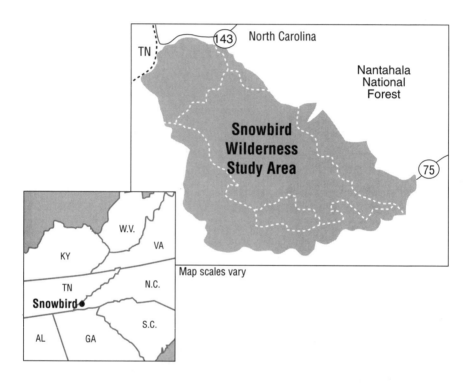

SNOWBIRD WILDERNESS STUDY AREA
Size: 8,490 acres.
Year designated: Not designated.
Public land unit: Nantahala National Forest.
Features: Waterfalls; trout streams; remote mountains.
Representative wildlife: Black bear; wild hogs; brook trout.
Wilderness map: The 1:24,000-scale Snowbird Area Trail map.
U.S.G.S. topographic maps: Big Junction; Marble; Santeetlah Creek.
County: Graham.
Information: Cheoah District Ranger, Robbinsville, NC 28711. (704) 479-6431.

Southern Nantahala Wilderness

Southern Nantahala Wilderness's 23,714 acres make it the third-largest national forest wilderness in the Southern Appalachians.

Southern Nantahala's centerpiece is Standing Indian Mountain, a 5,499-foot-high peak which gives visitors views of large expanses of nearly unbroken forest.

The wilderness lies in both Georgia and North Carolina. It was heavily logged in the early part of the 20th Century. The basin that surrounds much of the wilderness was owned by Ritter Lumber Co., which hauled out trees on a narrow-gauge railroad.

The Forest Service bought the land in 1920 as part of the Nantahala National Forest. But Ritter held timber rights to the land for 20 years. While most of the forest of red oak, chestnut oak, tulip-poplar and hickory is second-growth, scattered stands of old-growth hemlock and oak remain.

Here's how the state's Natural Heritage Program describes the North Carolina section: "Much of the slopes and ridge tops are covered by red oak-dominated forest. Eastern hemlock grow along the narrow creek ravines on the mountain's eastern flank and cove forests and northern hardwood forests cover the ravines of the low and mid-elevation slopes."

The Eastern Continental Divide splits Southern Nantahala. The wilderness contains the headwaters of the Nantahala River, which flows west in North Carolina to the Tennessee River; and the Tallulah River, which flows south through Georgia to the Savannah River.

Numerous springs, waterfalls and sheer cliffs, some several hundred feet high, give the wilderness a distinctive character. Most of the area is above 3,000 feet in elevation. This is one of the wettest areas in the East; part of the adjacent Coweeta area averages 82 inches of rain and snow a year.

Southern Nantahala is also a home of the federally endangered Indiana bat and the state endangered bog turtle. A few of these small, four-inch-long, mud-loving reptiles live in high mountain bogs.

Peregrine falcons have been released here. The birds may be seen gliding over the high peaks and cliffs.

Black bear abound here. The North Carolina section lies within a bear sanctuary, which means that hunting is banned. Bear sign is not hard to find. Bears often shred wooden trail markers with their claws.

The Appalachian Trail traverses Southern Nantahala for 24 miles. It enters the wilderness at Blue Ridge Gap on the 11,770-acre Georgia side and at Mooney Gap on the 11,944-acre North Carolina side.

As in other wildernesses, the Appalachian Trail's shelters and trail markers remain intact. They were deemed by Congress to be compatible with wilderness designation and necessary for the health and safety of hikers using the trail.

Four other maintained trails totalling nearly 19 miles tie to the Appalachian Trail.

The Georgia section lies between Hiawassee and Clayton. The North Carolina section is about 20 miles southwest of Franklin.

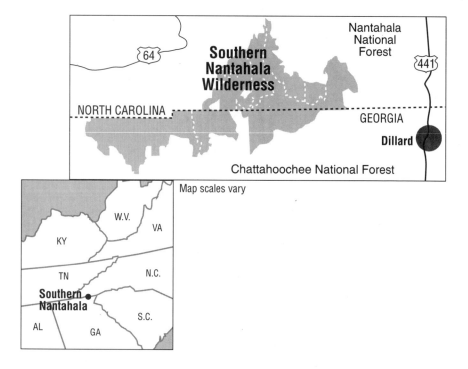

SOUTHERN NANTAHALA WILDERNESS
Size: 23,714 acres.
Year designated: 1984.
Public land units: Chattahoochee National Forest; Nantahala National Forest.
Features: Grass-heath balds; spruce-fir forests; high cliffs and steep valleys.
Representative wildlife: Black bear; peregrine falcon; bog turtle.
Wilderness map: The 1:24,000-scale Southern Nantahala Wilderness and Standing Indian Basin map.
U.S.G.S. topographic maps: (Georgia) Hightower Bald; Macedonia; (North Carolina) Rainbow Springs; Shooting Creek.
Counties: Rabun and Towns counties, Ga; Clay and Macon, N.C.
Information: Tusquitee Ranger District, Nantahala National Forest, 201 Woodland Drive, Murphy, NC 28906. (704) 837-5152. Wayah Ranger District, Nantahala National Forest, 80 Sloan Road, Franklin, NC 28734. (704) 524-6441. Tallulah Ranger District, Chattahoochee National Forest, Box 438, Clayton, GA 30525. (706) 782-3320.

The meadows or savannahs produce excellent grass; being watered by abundance of fine rivers, and brooks well stored with fish, otters and beavers;...There are likewise an incredible number of buffaloes, bears, deer, panthers, wolves, foxes, raccoons and opposums...There are a vast number of lesser sort of game, such as rabbits, squirrels of several sorts, and many other animals beside turkeys, geese, ducks of several kinds, partridges, pheasants, and an infinity of other birds....

—*Lieut. Henry Timberlake's Memoirs*, 1756-1765. The Watauga Press, Johnson City, Tenn., 1927, Samuel C. Williams, editor. He was describing what is now Tennessee around the lower Tennessee River Valley.

SOUTH CAROLINA

Ellicott Rock Wilderness

Towering hemlock trees, deep gorges and the pristine Chattooga River underscore Ellicott Rock's wild beauty.

The Chattooga forms the centerpiece of the 8,274-acre wilderness nestled in the corner of Georgia, North Carolina and South Carolina.

The river spills out of its headwaters in North Carolina, cascading through rock cliffs and over huge boulders. Native brook trout lurk in its greenish pools. Trilliums and violets embroider the stream banks.

The Chattooga, a 50-mile-long National Wild and Scenic River, forms the border between Georgia and South Carolina in a five-mile journey through the wilderness. The terrain is steep; the highest point, 3,672-foot-high Glade Mountain, stands 1,400 feet above the Chattooga gorge.

The Ellicott Rock area abounds in history. Archeologists believe that a Cherokee Indian village known as "Chattooga Old Town" was located at the mouth of the West Fork of the Chattooga.

The wilderness draws its name from surveyor Andrew Ellicott. In 1813, he used a large rock as a boundary marker for the intersection of the three states.

Most of the area was logged in the 1920s. The Forest Service in

1966 classified the present wilderness and land around it as a scenic area, protecting natural values.

When Ellicott Rock was designated in 1975, most of the original 3,332 acres lay in the Sumter National Forest in South Carolina. In 1984 the wilderness expanded in the Chattahoochee National Forest in Georgia to 2,021 acres and in the Nantahala National Forest in North Carolina to 3,394 acres. More than 90 percent of the visitors enter from the 2,859-acre South Carolina side.

Ellicott Rock gets more than 80 inches of rain and snow a year, making it a paradise for moisture-loving plants like mountain laurel and rhododendron. The nation's largest rosebay rhododendron — the shrub has rose-colored or purple flowers — lives here. It stands 40 feet high.

The ridges and upland slopes are covered with dogwood, hickory, chestnut oak and pitch pine. White pine and hemlocks flourish in the coves and along the streams. The Forest Service has determined Ellicott Rock potentially contains 4,630 acres of old-growth trees,

Rhododendron-bordered stream rushes toward Chattooga River in Ellicott Rock Wilderness.

Large-flowered trillium shows its beauty in Ellicott Rock Wilderness.

about half the wilderness.

In spring, the woods are rife with sweet white violets, bloodroot, rue anenome, wood anenome, jack-in-the-pulpit, painted trillium and large-flowered trillium, to name a few. A rare plant, the Oconee bell, is found here as are two federally endangered plants, rock gnome lichen and small whorled pogonia.

Visitors will find a rare structure: A log bridge over the East Fork to reduce erosion caused by hikers climbing the steep banks. The wilderness has four trails totalling 18.5 miles.

The wilderness is about 15 miles north of Walhalla, S.C., and about 10 miles southeast of Highlands, N.C.

ELLICOTT ROCK WILDERNESS
Size: 8,274 acres.
Years designated: 1975; 1984.
Public land units: Chattahoochee National Forest; Nantahala National Forest; Sumter National Forest.
Features: Steep terrain, gorges, Chattooga River.
Representative wildlife: Black bear, brook trout, songbirds.
Wilderness map: The 1:24,000-scale Ellicott Rock Wilderness map.
U.S.G.S. topographic maps: Cashiers; Satolah; Tamassee.
Counties: Rabun County, GA; Jackson, Macon counties, NC; Oconee County, SC.
Information: Tallulah Ranger District, Chattahoochee National Forest, Chechero/Savannah Street, Box 438, Clayton, GA 30525. (706) 782-3320. Highlands Ranger District, Nantahala National Forest, 2010 Flat Mountain Road, Highlands, NC 28741. (704) 526-3765. Andrew Pickens Ranger District, Sumter National Forest, 112 Andrew Pickens Circle, Mountain Rest, SC 29664. (864) 638-9568.

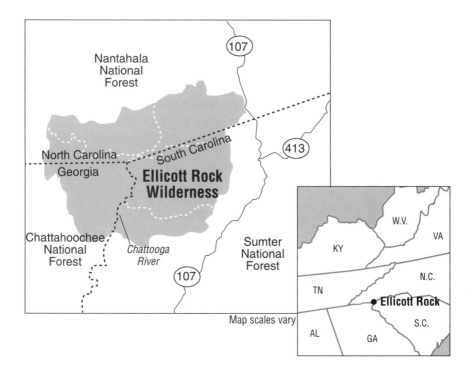

After crossing this delightful brook and mead, the land rises again with sublime magnificence, and I am led over hills and vales, groves and high forests, vocal with the melody of the feathered songsters, the snow-white cascades glittering on the sides of the distant hills.

—Naturalist William Bartram, describing his walk through northern Georgia in 1775. From *The Travels of William Bartram*, edited by Francis Harper, Yale University Press, New Haven, Conn. 1958.

147

TENNESSEE

Bald River Gorge Wilderness

Bald River Gorge Wilderness lies deep in the Unicoi Mountains, conveying a sense of remoteness and wildness.

Bordered by roadless areas of the Cherokee National Forest, the wilderness lies a few miles southwest of the Citico Creek-Joyce Kilmer-Slickrock wilderness complex.

Bald River Gorge follows the gorge of the Bald River, a plunging, cascading stream that spills into the Tellico River. The river's glass-clear pools hold brook, rainbow and brown trout.

Designated in 1984, the wilderness covers 3,721 acres of sometimes steep terrain. The elevation ranges from 1,200 feet at the 120-foot-high Bald River Falls to 3,000 feet on Gravel Stand Top.

Yellow and white pines along with chestnut and scarlet oaks dominate the ridge tops while hardwood cove trees — tulip-poplar, birch and beech — rise from rhododendron and mountain laurel. Last logged in the 1920s, the forest now is about 60 to 70 years old.

The lone trail in the wilderness begins on Forest Service road 210, at the Bald River Falls, and follows for 4.7 miles the east side of the stream to Forest Service road 126 near the Holly Flats Recreation Area.

Hikers may see woodland sunflowers, spiked lobelia, smooth aster and cardinal flower.

149

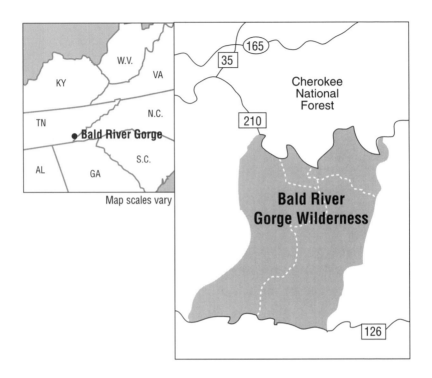

Map scales vary

Bald River Gorge Wilderness is about seven miles east of Tellico Plains in southeastern Tennessee.

BALD RIVER GORGE WILDERNESS
Size: 3,721 acres.
Year designated: 1984.
Public land unit: Cherokee National Forest.
Features: Cascading mountain stream within a steep gorge.
Representative wildlife: Brown and rainbow trout; wild hog; white-tailed deer.
Wilderness map: None.
U.S.G.S. topographic map: Bald River.
County: Monroe.
Information: Tellico Ranger District, Route 3, Tellico River Road, Tellico Plains, TN 37385. (423) 253-2520.

Frothing water cascades over rocks in Bald River Gorge Wilderness.

Big Frog Wilderness
Little Frog Mountain Wilderness

A sanctuary for black bears and rare plants, Big Frog Wilderness forms the northern segment of a wilderness complex of nearly 44,000 acres.

Big Frog adjoins Georgia's Cohutta Wilderness to the south; an 89-acre segment of Big Frog lies in Georgia's Chattahoochee National Forest.

To the north, across the Ocoee River and U.S. 64, Little Frog Mountain Wilderness contributes to the mosaic of wilderness and national forest lands with 4,666 acres of mountain forest.

Isolated and lightly used, Big Frog captures the essence of Southern Appalachian wilderness. Big Frog was rated the highest of Cherokee National Forest roadless areas for wilderness attributes during the second RARE II (Roadless Area Review and Evaluation) process in the 1970s.

The 8,082-acre area covers a rugged landscape topped by Big

151

Fall-blooming sunflower favors sunny area in Big Frog Wilderness.

Frog Mountain, at 4,224 feet the highest point in the wilderness. The second-growth forest of hardwoods such as hickory, white oak and northern red oak and Virginia pine approaches a climax forest; tree ages range from 60 to 100 years. Selective cutting of trees occurred about 30 years ago.

Wildlife is diverse. Black bear are abundant; Big Frog is part of a state bear preserve. Other animals include wild hog, wild turkey, gray fox and rabbit.

A rainbow of wildflowers color the forest floor. Birdsfoot violet, rue anemone, wild bleeding heart, white snakeroot, yellow star grass, downy false foxglove are among the more common. Rarer plants include Dutchman's pipe and purple flowering raspberry.

Big Frog has 10 hiking trails that cover nearly 26 miles. The first trails were built by the Civilian Conservation Corps in the 1930s.

Still, few people other than hunters venture into Big Frog.

To the north, Little Frog Mountain is more accessible.

Unlike the steep terrain of Big Frog, Little Frog Mountain consists of a long ridge with elevations running from 2,200 to 3,322 feet. The rolling low mountains lie under a second-growth forest of hardwoods and yellow and white pines. Underneath the canopy is an understory of sourwood, dogwood and flame azalea.

Two trails totalling 9.5 miles traverse the wilderness.

Both Little Frog Mountain and Big Frog are about 30 miles east of Cleveland in the southeastern corner of Tennessee. Both wildernesses are in Polk County.

BIG FROG WILDERNESS
Size: 8,082 acres.
Years designated: 1984, 1986.
Public land units: Cherokee National Forest; Chattahoochee National Forest.
Features: Maturing forest; isolated mountains.

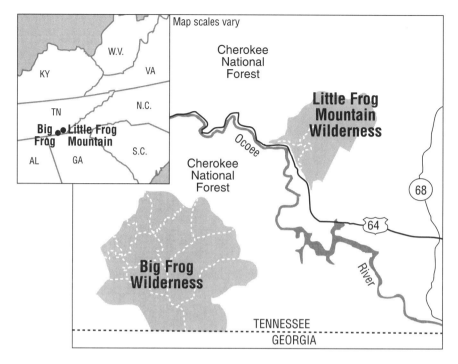

Representative wildlife: Black bear; gray fox; wild hog.
Wilderness map: The 1:31,680-scale Cohutta and Big Frog Wilderness map.
U.S.G.S. topographic maps: Caney Creek; Ducktown; Epworth; Hemp Top.
County: Polk.
Information: Ocoee Ranger District, Cherokee National Forest, Route 1, Box 3480, Benton, TN 37307. (423) 338-5201; Cohutta Ranger District, Chattahoochee National Forest, 401 Old Ellijay Road, Chatsworth, GA 30705. (706) 695-6737.

LITTLE FROG MOUNTAIN WILDERNESS
Size: 4,666 acres.
Year designated: 1986.
Public land unit: Cherokee National Forest.
Features: Rolling mountains; maturing forest.
Representative wildlife: White-tailed deer, wild turkey, grouse.
Wilderness map: None.
U.S.G.S. topographic map: Ducktown.
County: Polk.
Information: Ocoee Ranger District, Route 1, Box 3480, Benton, TN 37307. (423) 338-5201.

Big Laurel Branch Wilderness
Pond Mountain Wilderness

These wildernesses overlook Watauga Lake, providing a southern version of a North Woods setting in the Tennessee mountains.

Big Laurel Branch Wilderness hunkers over the northern shore of the lake while Pond Mountain Wilderness buttresses the southern flank.

Combined, the two wildernesses safeguard 13,261 acres of the Cherokee National Forest. Both were designated in 1986.

Big Laurel is an elongated wilderness. The Appalachian Trail runs for about five miles along the spine of the wilderness. At periodic openings, hikers get striking views southward across the lake toward Pond Mountain.

Steep and narrow ridges separate hollows; streams make sudden drops and slides. Cliffs hang over the edge of the lake; at the western edge, the sheer rock walls of Wilbur Lake give a fjord-like appearance.

Big Laurel's mountains rise 1,400 feet above the lake. Yellow pine, white pines and hemlocks cover the rugged landscape studded with rock outcroppings. The forest now is about 70 to 80 years old.

Across the man-made lake, Pond Mountain's 4,329-foot-high peak dominates its namesake wilderness.

At the core of Pond Mountain is the previously designated Watauga Scenic Area, which contains stands of old-growth trees in its upper reaches.

Pond Mountain's steep slopes, many with an incline greater than 60 percent, hold upland hardwoods and yellow pine with a smattering of hemlocks. Rhododendron, Fraser sedge, mountain mint and Allegheny cliff fern live in the wilderness as do wildflowers such as rue anemone and violets.

Several waterfalls splash through the Laurel Fork Gorge area along the western edge of the wilderness.

Some 6.6 miles of the Appalachian Trail traverse Pond Mountain wilderness along with six miles of the Pond Mountain trail and one mile of the Watauga Scenic trail.

154

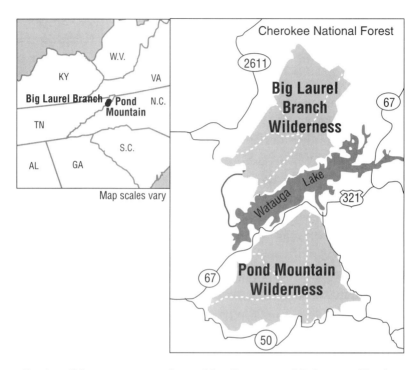

Both wildernesses are about 25 miles east of Johnson City in east Tennessee.

BIG LAUREL BRANCH WILDERNESS
Size: 6,332 acres.
Year designated: 1986.
Public land unit: Cherokee National Forest.
Features: Steep ridges; fjord-like appearance.
Representative wildlife: White-tailed deer, wild turkey, grouse.
Wilderness map: None.
U.S.G.S. topographic maps: Carter; Elizabethton; Watauga Dam.
Counties: Carter; Johnson.
Information: Watauga Ranger District, Route 9, Box 2235, Elizabethton, TN 37643. (423) 542-2942.

POND MOUNTAIN WILDERNESS
Size: 6,929 acres.
Year designated: 1986.
Public land unit: Cherokee National Forest.

155

Features: Rock cliffs; secluded hollows.
Representative wildlife: White-tailed deer; raccoon; pileated woodpecker.
Wilderness map: None.
U.S.G.S. Topographic maps: Elizabethton; Watauga Dam.
Counties: Carter; Johnson.
Information: Watauga Ranger District, Route 9, Box 2235, Elizabethton, TN 37643. (423) 542-2942.

Citico Creek Wilderness

Citico Creek Wilderness arose from charred stumps in the 1930s to a maturing forest that's becoming wilder each year.

The wilderness is a premier example of how a Southern Appalachian forest can recover from massive logging in less than a lifetime.

Citico Creek became a 16,226-acre wilderness in the Unicoi Mountains in 1984. The boundary runs along the eastern edge of the Cherokee National Forest, next to the North Carolina state line.

Joyce Kilmer-Slickrock Wilderness borders the eastern edge of Citico Creek. Together, the two wildernesses form a block of wild lands of more than 33,000 acres.

Black bear and wild hogs roam the steep mountains and isolated valleys of Citico Creek. The wilderness is a state bear sanctuary. Brown and rainbow trout swim the chill waters of the North Fork and South Fork of the Citico Creek itself; brook trout live in some of the smaller streams.

At the beginning of the 20th Century, Citico Creek remained a virtual primeval wilderness. In 1922, the Babcock Land and Timber Co. bought the land and began logging. That was about seven years after the company started felling trees in the adjacent Slickrock area in North Carolina.

The intensive logging razed the original forest, leaving the mountains scalped except for occasional scraggly trees that the loggers had passed over.

Uncontrolled wildfires swept over Citico Creek in 1925, an extremely dry year. The fires, perhaps started by sparks from passing logging trains, ignited the branches and other woody debris left on the mountainsides.

The fires forced Babcock to stop logging except in the Doublecamp Branch area in the northern part of what is now wilderness. Logging ceased entirely in 1929.

Afterward, several families moved in to farm the cleared areas and pastured their cattle in the higher elevations.

In 1935, the Forest Service acquired Citico Creek. The scarred mountains grew back in yellow pines, scarlet oak and hemlocks. Nurtured by rain and snowfall amounts of up to 80 inches a year, a second-growth forest now has reclaimed 99 percent of the land.

Only a few small stands of old-growth forest remain among the second-growth mixture of upland hardwoods, cove hardwoods and pine. One old-growth pocket is a 187-acre beech-maple forest in the Falls Branch area; another is a 200-acre hemlock-hardwood stand between Glenn Gap and the headwaters of Indian Valley Branch.

The elevations in the steeply sloped wilderness range from 1,400

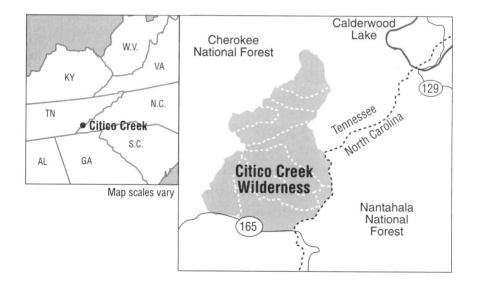

to 4,600 feet at the crest of the Unicoi Mountains, which divide Citico Creek from Joyce Kilmer-Slickrock. The slopes create numerous waterfalls, including 80-foot-high Falls Branch Falls. The waterfall is just inside the southern boundary of the wilderness, just off the scenic Cherohala Skyway between Tellico Plains, Tenn., and Robbinsville, N.C.

A network of 13 trails totalling nearly 60 miles lace Citico Creek and stitch it to Joyce Kilmer-Slickrock.

The wilderness lies about 10 miles southwest of the southwestern tip of the Great Smoky Mountains National Park and about 30 miles east of Athens in southeast Tennessee. It is in Monroe County.

CITICO CREEK WILDERNESS
Size: 16,226 acres.
Year designated: 1984.
Public land unit: Cherokee National Forest.
Features: Steep terrain; sheer bluffs; numerous waterfalls.
Representative wildlife: Black bear; wild hog; white-tailed deer.
Wilderness map: The 1:24,000-scale Joyce Kilmer-Slickrock Wilderness and Citico Creek Wilderness map.
U.S.G.S topographic maps: Big Junction; White Oak Flats.
County: Monroe.
Information: Tellico Ranger District, Route 3, Tellico River Road, Tellico Plains, TN 37385. (423) 253-2520.

Cohutta Wilderness

See Georgia section for a description of Cohutta Wilderness.

Cumberland Gap National Historical Park

See Kentucky section for a description of Cumberland Gap National Historical Park.

Gee Creek Wilderness

A cascading trout stream and sheer rock cliffs form the centerpiece of this small wilderness.

The stream, Gee Creek, tumbles out of a small gorge covered

with rhododendron and hemlocks in the Cherokee National Forest.

The 1.4-mile Gee Creek trail follows the creek up the increasingly narrow gorge. Be prepared to make several crossings as the trail ascends the ridges that parallel the gorge.

Hikers can see evidence of Gee Creek's history as a quartzite ore quarry.

In the early 1900s, the Tennessee Copper Co. mined the ore, loaded it in wagons and hauled it to the nearby Wetmore community. The ore was then taken to nearby Copperhill, a mining center, where the ore was used for construction.

Nature has healed the blasting and mining that took place along Gee Creek as well as the logging. Lumberjacks last entered Gee Creek 70 to 90 years ago. A maturing forest of white pines, northern red oak, white oak and tulip-poplar now envelops the wilderness.

In 1975, Congress designated 2,493 acres as wilderness, Tennessee's smallest. Gee Creek is sparsely used, drawing only sev-

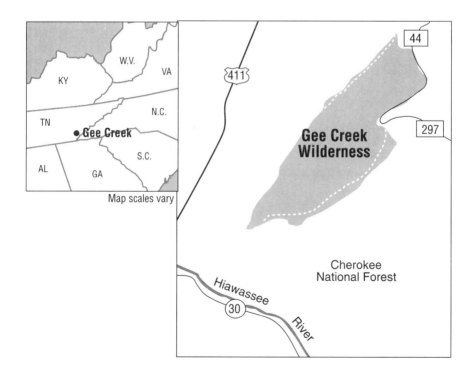

eral hundred people a year.

The wilderness is about 15 miles southeast of Athens in southeastern Tennessee.

GEE CREEK WILDERNESS
Size: 2,493 acres.
Year designated: 1975.
Public land unit: Cherokee National Forest.
Features: Waterfalls and rock cliffs.
Representative wildlife: Black bear; white-tailed deer, grouse.
Wilderness map: None.
U.S.G.S. topographic maps: Etowah; McFarland; Mecca; Oswald Dome.
Counties: McMinn; Monroe; Polk.
Information: Hiawassee Ranger District, Drawer D, Etowah, TN 37331. (423) 263-5486.

Great Smoky Mountains National Park Proposed Wilderness

See North Carolina section for a description of Great Smoky Mountains National Park Proposed Wilderness.

Joyce Kilmer-Slickrock Wilderness

See North Carolina section for a description of Joyce Kilmer-Slickrock Wilderness.

Pond Mountain Wilderness

See Big Laurel Branch Wilderness for a description of Pond Mountain Wilderness.

Sampson Mountain Wilderness

Sampson Mountain, an 7,992-acre wilderness overlooking the farm lands of East Tennessee, holds one of the highest cascades in the Eastern United States.

The cascade is Buckeye Falls, which spills 475 feet out of the upper reaches of Clark Creek in the southern part of the wilderness.

Sampson Mountain Wilderness sign.

The highest waterfall in the East is 800-foot Whitewater Falls in the Nantahala National Forest in North Carolina.

The waterfall isn't the only attraction of Sampson Mountain. The wilderness harbors steep, open ridges, secluded hollows and clear mountain streams. Elevations range from 2,200 to 3,800 feet.

Wilderness values rank high in Sampson Mountain. The area tied with Big Frog Wilderness as having the highest wilderness rating of any area in Tennessee in the RARE II study.

Since relatively few people venture into Sampson Mountain, the opportunity

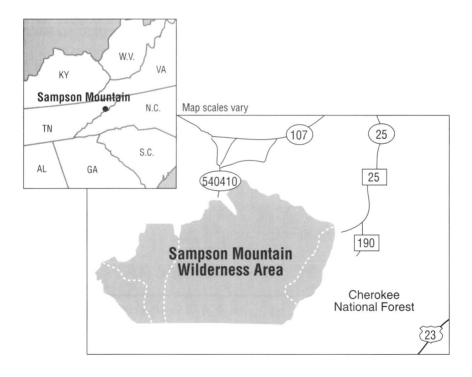

161

for solitude is high. The isolation and maturing hardwood and pine forest provide black bear habitat. The wilderness is a state bear sanctuary.

A devastating fire in 1952 burned much of the area to the mineral soil, resulting in poor quality trees as measured by their worth as timber.

The wilderness now has a second-growth forest of table mountain pine, yellow poplar and yellow birch as well as about 536 acres of old-growth forest.

Sampson Mountain has four trails totalling 7.2 miles.

The wilderness is about 25 miles southwest of Johnson City in East Tennessee and about 15 miles east of Greeneville.

SAMPSON MOUNTAIN WILDERNESS
Size: 7,992 acres.
Year designated: 1986.
Public land unit: Cherokee National Forest.
Features: Contains one of highest cascades in East.
Representative wildlife: Black bear; fox; ruffed grouse.
Wilderness map: None.
U.S.G.S. topographic maps: Flag Pond; Graystone; Telford.
Counties: Greene; Unicoi; Washington.
Information: Unaka Ranger District, 1205 N. Main Street, Erwin, TN 37650. (423) 743-3116.

Unaka Mountain Wilderness

Unaka Mountain Wilderness overlooks hundreds of square miles of coves and valleys, farms and towns from a platform in the Cherokee National Forest.

The north-facing wilderness offers panoramic views from almost any point, spreading across the lower face of 4,957-foot-high Unaka Mountain.

At the highest points of the wilderness, above 4,000 feet, visitors can look west to see 5,516-foot-high Big Bald Mountain.

Looking north, Buffalo Mountain looms behind the town of Erwin on the valley floor. Looking east, Roan Mountain and Pond Moun-

Rime ice, also called frozen fog, streaks up the side of Unaka Mountain Wilderness.

tain stand out in the checkerboard of private lands and public lands.

The 4,496-acre wilderness is partly encircled by Forest Service road 230, which connects to Tennessee 107 and 395. In rainy or icy weather, better take a four-wheel-drive vehicle.

The wilderness climbs more than 2,000 feet on Unaka Mountain's north face. It ascends from 2,430 feet at the Rock Creek Recreation Area on the northwestern corner, to 4,840 feet at the Pleasant Garden overlook beside Forest Service road 230.

Higher, along the crest of Unaka Mountain itself, the Appalachian Trail courses along the state line just south of the wilderness boundary.

More than 10 waterfalls cascade 20 feet or more, including 60-foot-high Red Fork Falls near the eastern boundary.

The core of the wilderness is the former Unaka Mountain Scenic Area, perched on a ridge that descends sharply from the crest of Unaka Mountain. A parking lot lies a few hundred yards from the Forest Service road 230.

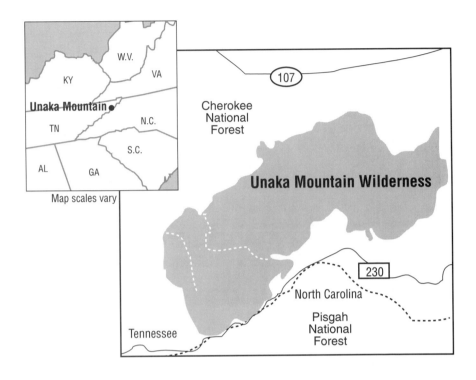

At the parking lot is Rattlesnake Ridge Trail, which ends in 3.8 miles at the Rock Creek Recreation Area. In all, Unaka Mountain has four trails totalling 13.6 miles.

Located in East Tennessee, Unaka Mountain lies about 20 miles southwest of Johnson City.

UNAKA MOUNTAIN WILDERNESS
Size: 4,496 acres.
Year designated: 1986.
Public land unit: Cherokee National Forest.
Features: Old-growth hemlocks; waterfalls.
Representative wildlife: New England cottontail; raven; great crested flycatcher; timber rattlesnake.
Wilderness map: None.
U.S.G.S. topographic maps: Huntdale; Unicoi. Counties: Unicoi.
Information: Unaka District Ranger, Cherokee National Forest, 1205 N. Main St., Erwin, TN 37650. (423) 743-3116.

164

Back when I wuz a boy, people from around here would go to th' White Top Mountain. That 'uz purty wild up there then. And they was some big wolves up there, called timber wolves. An' men 'ud go up there an' camp and hunt 'em. They'd take dogs...It 'ud take a mighty good dog to fight a wolf. Gener'ly, it takes two or three dogs to kill a grown wolf...Well, they went up there to hunt wolves, but their dogs, a big pack uv 'um, got after a panther an' treed it...An' then (they) went to th' tree, them fellers did, an' shot th' panther out....

—William Maisten Paisley, Mouth of Wilson, Va., recounting the Mount Rogers area, in *Southern Appalachia*, 1885-1915, by Roy Edwin Thomas, McFarland & Co. Inc., Jefferson, N.C., 1991.

VIRGINIA

Barbours Creek Wilderness
Shawvers Run Wilderness

Wedged between mountain forests and small farms, Barbours Creek and Shawvers Run protect two forested enclaves near the West Virginia line.

The two wildernesses lie within a mile of each other in the Jefferson National Forest, straddling either side of Potts Mountain, the area's dominant landmark.

Barbours Creek spills across 5,382 acres on the mountain's southeastern slope. Smaller at 3,467 acres, Shawvers Run Wilderness lies on Potts Mountain's western slope. Both were carved out in 1988 from a roadless study area that covered 15,000 acres.

Located about 35 miles northwest of Roanoke, the wildernesses likely will remain largely the haunts of hunters and fishermen. Together they have only one developed trail, located in Barbours Creek.

The Lipes Branch trail in Barbours Creek begins at The Pines campground. The 2.3-mile trail goes up the slope to the ridge overlooking the wilderness. The elevation gain of 2,100 feet terminates at the 3,800-foot flat ridge that helps make up Potts Mountain.

Named for the stream that tumbles out of the west end of the wilderness, Shawvers Run attracts few visitors other than local fishermen and bear hunters.

Shawvers Run lies in a deep, oblong valley. The highest point in the wilderness is 3,800 feet on the southern border at Hanging Rock, a rock outcropping that juts over an expansive valley. The rock provides a panoramic, northerly view into the hardwood forest.

Four acres of Barbours Creek and 102 acres of Shawvers Run wildernesses lie in the adjoining George Washington National Forest. The wildernesses are about 35 miles northwest of Roanoke in western Virginia.

BARBOURS CREEK WILDERNESS
Size: 5,382 acres.
Year designated: 1988.
Public land units: Jefferson National Forest; George Washington National Forest.
Features: Elongated ridge above steeply sloped mountain.
Representative wildlife: White-tailed deer, wild turkey, brook trout.
Wilderness map: Black-and-white brochure.
U.S.G.S. topographic maps: Jordan Mines; Potts Creek.

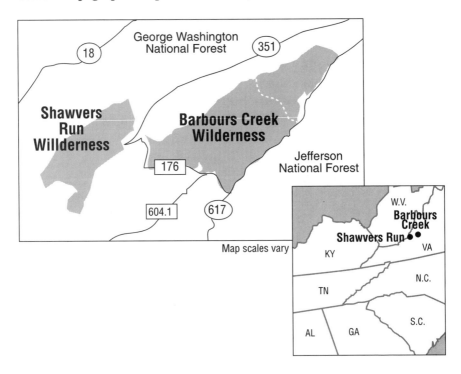

168

County: Craig.
Information: New Castle Ranger District, Jefferson National Forest, Box 246, New Castle, VA 24127. (540) 864-5195.

SHAWVERS RUN WILDERNESS
Size: 3,467 acres.
Year designated: 1988.
Public land units: Jefferson National Forest; George Washington National Forest.
Features: Steep valley draining two creeks, Shawvers Run and Valley Branch.
Representative wildlife: Black bear; white-tailed deer, brook trout.
Wilderness map: Black-and-white brochure.
U.S.G.S. topographic map: Potts Creek.
County: Craig.
Information: New Castle Ranger District, Box 246, New Castle, VA 24127. (540) 864-5195.

Beartown Wilderness

Beartown forms a rugged outpost in the Jefferson National Forest, a striking counterpoint to the rolling farmland in nearby adjacent valleys.

The wilderness is accessible both by the Appalachian Trail, which runs along the southern boundary of Beartown for three miles, and an unimproved road on its southeastern boundary.

No maintained trails lead into the interior of the 5,609-acre wilderness. Those who want to enter Beartown must search out old roadbeds or bushwhack their way along steep terrain.

Beartown is one of three Virginia wildernesses that have no interior trails and are likely to have the least human imprint over the years. The other two are Kimberling Creek and Shawvers Run.

Beartown's remoteness can be seen from the Appalachian Trail, particularly where the trail meets the rock shelter at Chestnut Mountain.

Here, one gets a grandstand view of the western Virginia mountains. The vista takes in Mount Rogers, at 5,729 feet the highest point in Virginia, across to the 4,500-foot-high ridge dotted with red spruce that marks Beartown's northern border.

To the east is a pastoral valley of white farmhouses, silos, beige and green farm fields. It's the Burke's Garden community.

The northeast corner of the wilderness holds an Appalachian bog, an ecosystem that's rapidly disappearing elsewhere because of development. Nearby beaver ponds are the headwaters for the streams that flow out of the wilderness.

A forest of red spruce and northern hardwoods and hemlocks covers the wilderness. Loggers got the last old-growth trees 50 to 60 years ago. Logging continued until the 1940s.

The maturing second-growth forest provides habitat for black bear, white-tailed deer, grouse and northern red flying squirrels, rare in southwest Virginia.

Other denizens include birds that nest in more northerly forests, among them the black-capped chickadee, red-breasted nuthatch and winter wren. The Beartown beetle, a species of ground beetle found nowhere else in the world, lives here.

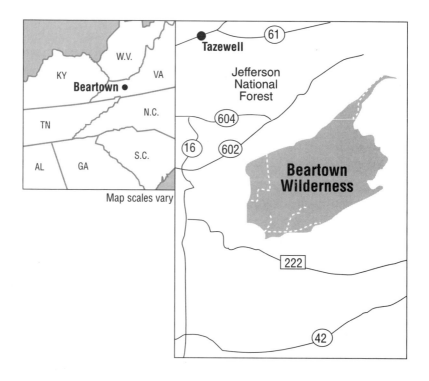

Beartown is about 25 miles northwest of Wytheville in western Virginia.

BEARTOWN WILDERNESS
Size: 5,609 acres.
Year designated: 1984.
Public land unit: Jefferson National Forest.
Features: Isolated mountain forest; Appalachian bog.
Representative wildlife: Black bear, white-tailed deer, beaver.
Wilderness map: Black-and-white folder.
U.S.G.S. topographic map: Hutchinson Rock.
County: Tazewell.
Information: Wythe Ranger District, 155 Sherwood Road, Wytheville, VA 24382. (540) 228-5551 or Blacksburg Ranger District, 110 Southpark Dr., Blacksburg, VA 24060. (540) 552-4641.

Cumberland Gap National Historical Park
See Kentucky section for a description of Cumberland Gap National Historical Park.

James River Face Wilderness
Thunder Ridge Wilderness
These two adjoining wildernesses in the Jefferson National Forest combine to make a single mountainous tract of almost 11,500 acres.

The northernmost, James River Face, overlooks the James River as it flows eastward from the mountains to coastal Virginia.

Separated only by a dirt road, Thunder Ridge lies directly south of James River Face.

James River Face-Thunder Ridge is one of the few places in the Southern Appalachians in which the Appalachian Trail runs the entire length of a wilderness. The Blue Ridge Parkway borders the eastern edge of both wildernesses, adding a buffer of National Park Service land.

The core of James River Face received wilderness protection in 1975, the first in the state. In 1984, Congress created Thunder Ridge, at 2,344 acres Virginia's smallest wilderness.

At the same time, Congress added 200 acres to James River Face to link it with Thunder Ridge.

James River Face spans nearly a half mile in elevation, beginning at 650 feet at the James River to 3,073 feet at Highcock Knob. The ascent continues in Thunder Ridge, reaching 3,800 feet in the southern tip of the wilderness. The steep, rough terrain made both areas difficult for logging, thus sparing much of the interior from timber cutting. The Forest Service estimates only five percent, mostly around the edges, was cut. That means that an old-growth forest covers most of the land.

Some of the trees are mammoth. One red oak measures eight feet nine inches around. Upland hardwoods and yellow pines grow on the higher slopes while the lower slopes harbor cove hardwoods, hemlocks and white pines.

Six maintained trails wind through the two wildernesses, includ-

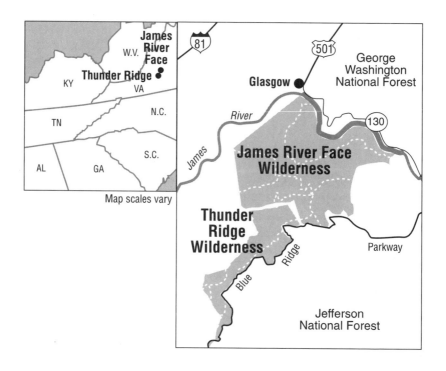

ing 14 miles of the Appalachian Trail.

James River Face and Thunder Ridge lie at the northern edge of the Jefferson National Forest, just east of Interstate 81 between Lexington and Lynchburg.

JAMES RIVER FACE WILDERNESS
Size: 8,886 acres.
Years designated: 1975, 1984.
Public land unit: Jefferson National Forest.
Features: Steep landscape; old-growth forest.
Representative wildlife: Black bear; fox; grouse.
Wilderness map: Black-and-white brochure.
U.S.G.S. topographic map: Snowden.
Counties: Bedford; Botetourt; Rockbridge.
Information: Glenwood Ranger District, Jefferson National Forest, Box 10, Natural Bridge Station, VA 24579. (540) 291-2188.

THUNDER RIDGE WILDERNESS
Size: 2,344 acres.
Year designated: 1984.
Public land unit: Jefferson National Forest.
Features: Old-growth forest.
Representative wildlife: Black bear; fox; grouse.
Wilderness map: Black-and-white brochure.
U.S.G.S. topographic maps: Arnold Valley; Snowden.
Counties: Bedford; Botetourt; Rockbridge.
Information: Glenwood Ranger District, Box 10, Natural Bridge Station, VA 24579. (540) 291-2188.

Kimberling Creek Wilderness

No trails, just 5,542 acres of forest distinguish Kimberling Creek Wilderness in the Jefferson National Forest.

It's an area of deep hollows, streams and woods made up of second-growth mixed hardwoods with white and yellow pines.

Elevations range from 2,282 feet to 3,200 feet on Hogback Mountain, the highest point in the wilderness.

Kimberling Creek lies less than a mile east of Interstate 77 in western Virginia, making it comparatively easy to get to. It's about

173

15 miles north of Wytheville and 10 miles south of the West Virginia state line.

The Appalachian Trail, after leaving the Beartown Wilderness to the west, swings just south of Kimberling Creek.

Kimberling Creek is bounded on the north by nine-mile-long Forest Service Road 640. The rocky, dirt road is suitable only for four-wheel drive vehicles.

KIMBERLING CREEK WILDERNESS
Size: 5,542 acres.
Year designated: 1984.
Public land unit: Jefferson National Forest.
Features: Rolling mountain terrain; deep hollows.
Representative wildlife: White-tailed deer, wild turkey, gray squirrel.
Wilderness map: Black-and-white brochure.
U.S.G.S. topographic map: Rocky Gap.
County: Bland.
Information: Wythe Ranger District, 155 Sherwood Forest Road, Wytheville, VA

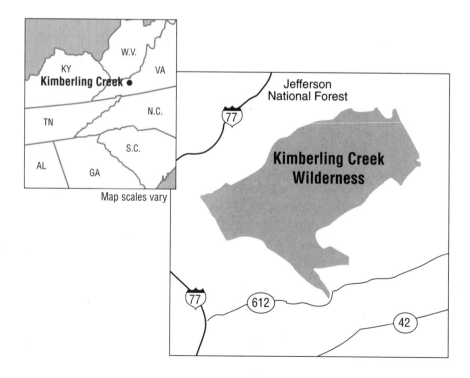

24382. (540) 228-5551 or Blacksburg Ranger District, 110 Southpark Dr., Blacksburg, VA 24060. (540) 552-4641.

Lewis Fork Wilderness
Little Wilson Creek Wilderness

Mount Rogers, the highest peak in Virginia, dominates the cloud-swathed meadows and forests of these two wildernesses.

The Lewis Fork Wilderness covers most of the 5,729-foot-high mountain, including its densely forested summit of red spruce and Fraser firs.

The Little Wilson Creek Wilderness lies about a mile to the east and envelops several peaks clustered around the flanks of Mount Rogers. Wilson Creek, a plunging, cascading stream, forms the western border of the wilderness.

The Mount Rogers area consists of towering mountains, grassy balds, swags and rocky outcrops thrust high into the Virginia sky. The combined size of the two wildernesses, designated in 1984, is 9,231 acres.

Snow field covers flank of Mount Rogers, Virginia's highest peak, in Lewis Fork Wilderness.

Lewis Fork and Little Wilson Creek form the centerpiece of the Mount Rogers National Recreation Area in the Jefferson National Forest. The 1966 designation by Congress decreed this area is to be managed for recreation, scenic, scientific and natural values. A limited amount of logging is allowed in the 115,736-acre national recreation area but not in the wildernesses.

Lying next to the Little Wilson Creek Wilderness is Grayson Highlands State Park, covering 4,700 acres.

Long-distance and day hikers use the Appalachian Trail and local trails. Cross-country skiers take advantage of Mount Rogers' abundant snowfall in winter. The area gets 60 to 80 inches of snow a year. The weather is unpredictable and dangerous around Mount Rogers. For that reason, hikers should carry cold-weather clothing, additional food and emergency supplies.

Though deep in the South, the climate is more like that of New England. A northern hardwood forest, a mixture of trees such as yellow birch, sugar maple and black cherry, covers the mountain slopes.

The Fraser fir trees on the summit of Mount Rogers have begun to show signs of decline from an exotic insect pest. The pest, the balsam woolly adelgid, began killing firs in North Carolina and Tennessee in the 1960s.

Logging and subsequent fires devastated the area in the early 1900s, leaving scarred, blackened slopes. The second-growth forest, now about 80 years old, has returned.

Wildlife has returned to the renewed forest. Ravens and hawks scan the forest for prey. Once extirpated, black bears returned in the 1980s. The Virginia Department of Game and Inland Fisheries trapped bears around the Shenandoah National Park and released 80 in the Mount Rogers area.

Visitors will see the mixture of two distinct eras that shaped the history of Mount Rogers.

The mountain was named for William Barton Rogers at his death in 1883. He was Virginia's first state geologist and founder of the Massachusetts Institute of Technology.

The wilderness areas give a glimpse into pre-settlement times when the original forest covered the western Virginia mountains.

The era of human settlement can be seen in the open, grassy areas between the two wildernesses. The areas are called the Crest Zone, a remnant of the time when farmers created meadows for their livestock. Motorized vehicles are banned in the Crest Zone as they are in wilderness.

The Forest Service maintains the meadows by burning and by letting cattle and wild ponies graze. Forest officials remind that the ponies are not domesticated, so they shouldn't be approached or handled.

Mount Rogers lies in southwestern Virginia, about midway between Bristol and Interstate 77.

LEWIS FORK WILDERNESS
Size: 5,618 acres.
Year designated: 1984.
Public land unit: Jefferson National Forest.

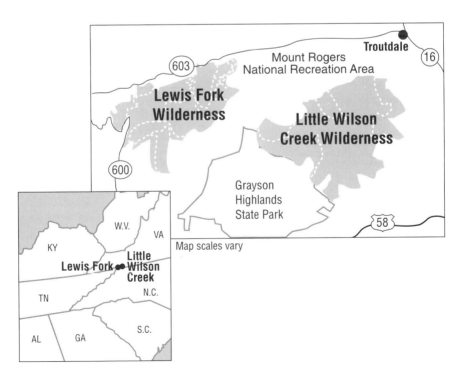

Features: Mount Rogers and its spruce-fir forest.
Representative wildlife: Black bear; northern flying squirrel.
Wilderness maps: The 1:24,000-scale Mount Rogers High Country and Wildernesses map; black-and-white brochure.
U.S.G.S. topographic map: Whitetop.
Counties: Grayson; Smyth.
Information: Mount Rogers National Recreation Area, Route 1, Box 303, Marion, VA 24354. (540) 783-5196.

LITTLE WILSON CREEK WILDERNESS
Size: 3,613 acres.
Year designated: 1984.
Public land unit: Jefferson National Forest.
Features: High peaks; native trout stream.
Representative wildlife: Black bear; red squirrel; ravens.
Wilderness maps: The 1:24,000-scale Mount Rogers High Country and Wildernesses map; black-and-white brochure.
U.S.G.S. topographic map: Troutdale.
Counties: Grayson; Smyth.
Information: Mount Rogers National Recreation Area, Route 1, Box 303, Marion, VA 24354. (540) 783-5196.

Little Dry Run Wilderness

One of Virginia's smaller wildernesses, Little Dry Run Wilderness acts as a bookend to Mount Rogers National Recreation area.

Like the Mount Rogers area, Little Dry Run was logged in the early 1900s. Some additional logging took place in the 1960s.

Today, Little Dry Run's 2,858 acres cover an upland hardwood forest at elevations ranging from 2,400 to 3,614 feet. The landscape consists not of towering mountains but of ridges and small streams.

A 2.6-mile foot trail runs through the wilderness from Forest Road 57 to U.S. 21. The Virginia Highlands Horse Trail follows the southern boundary of Little Dry Run for about five miles.

Comer's Rock, a large outcrop, is just south of the wilderness on Forest Road 57. The 4,102-foot-high perch on an observation platform treats visitors to a scenic tableau of farms, churches and pastures to the south.

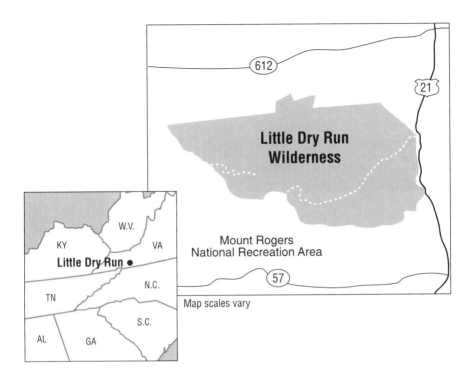

Map scales vary

LITTLE DRY RUN WILDERNESS
Size: 2,858 acres.
Year designated: 1984.
Public land unit: Jefferson National Forest.
Features: Upland hardwood forest; small streams.
Representative wildlife: White-tailed deer; wild turkey.
Wilderness map: Black-and-white brochure.
U.S.G.S. topographic map: Speedwell.
Counties: Wythe.
Information: Mount Rogers National Recreation Area, Route 1, Box 303, Marion, VA 24354. (540) 783-5196.

Little Wilson Creek Wilderness

See Lewis Fork Wilderness for a description of Little Wilson Creek Wilderness.

Mountain Lake Wilderness

Named for the only natural lake in the Virginia mountains, Mountain Lake Wilderness encompasses a diverse landscape that makes it a naturalist's delight.

Stands of old-growth hemlock and red spruce cover the slopes. Visitors can see a mountain bog, a wetland that is increasingly rare in the Southern Appalachians because of development.

The lake itself is not within the boundaries of the 11,113-acre wilderness but is about five miles south. It was formed when a rock slide dammed a small stream thousands of years ago at the north end of the 3,875-foot-high valley.

Mountain Lake Wilderness sits on the Eastern Continental Divide, meaning some of its streams flow to the Gulf of Mexico while others flow to the Atlantic Ocean.

A loop trail, one of several in the wilderness, takes hikers to a remnant old-growth stand in a ravine of War Branch Spur. The trail also leads to the nearby War Spur Overlook, the cliff that looks out to the north and northeastern parts of the wilderness.

The bog consisting of a soft sphagnum moss lies between the War Branch Spur area in the central part of the wilderness and the Appalachian Trail to the north. The trail runs beside several rocky outcroppings, giving hikers a view of the Little Mountain area. A 2,721-acre tract in West Virginia was added to the wilderness in 1988.

Biologists have catalogued 45 species of mammals and more than 70 species of birds in the Mountain Lake area. Wildflowers like Indian pipe, teaberry and fire pink carpet the ground along with ferns and blueberry bushes.

Five trails totalling 10.8 miles criss-cross the wilderness.

One notable fact: Virginia's lowest temperature ever, 30 degrees below zero, was recorded in 1985 just outside the wilderness.

Mountain Lake is about 20 miles north of Blacksburg.

MOUNTAIN LAKE WILDERNESS
Size: 11,113 acres.
Years designated: 1984; 1988.

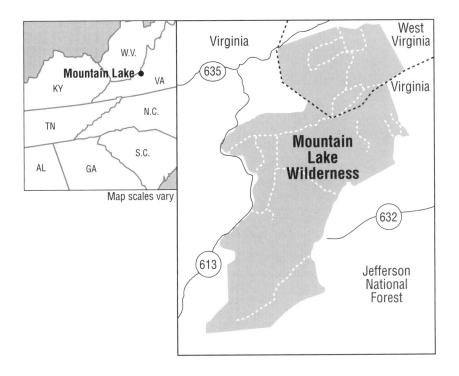

Public land unit: Jefferson National Forest.
Features: Stand of old-growth forest; Appalachian bog.
Representative wildlife: Black bear; white-tailed deer; deep forest birds like warblers. **Wilderness map:** Black-and-white brochure.
U.S.G.S. topographic maps: Eggleston; Interior; Newport; Waiteville.
Counties: Craig, Giles counties, VA; Monroe County, WVA.
Information: Blacksburg Ranger District, 110 Southpark Dr., Blacksburg, VA 24060. (540) 552-4641.

Peters Mountain Wilderness

A small mountain bog, a rare plant and the Appalachian Trail distinguish Peters Mountain Wilderness.

The bog is at the head of Pine Branch Swamp near the crest of Peters Mountain, a 3,956-foot high mountain in the Jefferson National Forest.

The bog contains cinnamon fern, sphagnum moss and sundew, a

181

Snow forms cast of rabbit tracks in Peters Mountain Wilderness.

plant that attracts insects to its sticky leaves, traps them and digests them as food.

Several miles away, on a secluded tract outside the wilderness, is one of the rarest plants in the world. It is the Peters Mountain mallow, whose numbers were down to three wild plants in the early 1990s. The mallow requires fire for regeneration of its seeds. Recent prescribed burns have increased the number of plants to about 200.

The Appalachian Trail passes through the 3,328-acre wilderness. It threads along the ridge line that marks the border between Virginia and West Virginia, before descending along Pine Swamp Branch, a total of two miles.

The trail leads to the Pine Swamp Shelter near the bottom of Peters Mountain, a few hundred yards from State Road 635.

Loggers last cut the Peters Mountain area in the 1920s and 1930s. All that is left of the original timber is a 10-acre stand of old-growth hemlocks.

A maturing upland oak forest of yellow poplar, chestnut oak, hickory and yellow pine dominate the steep, southeast-facing slopes with an understory of blueberry, mountain laurel and greenbriar. Wilderness designation came in 1984.

The wilderness is in western Virginia about 20 miles northwest of Blacksburg.

PETERS MOUNTAIN WILDERNESS
Size: 3,328 acres.
Year designated: 1984.
Public land unit: Jefferson National Forest.
Features: Appalachian bog; old-growth hemlock trees.
Representative wildlife: Black bear; white-tailed deer, wild turkey.

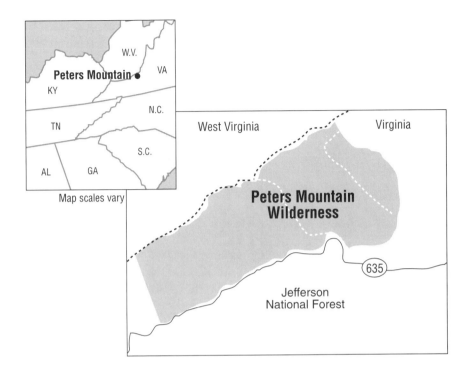

Wilderness map: Black-and-white brochure.
U.S.G.S. topographic maps: Interior; Lindside.
County: Giles.
Information: Blacksburg Ranger District, 110 Southpark Drive, Blacksburg, VA 24060. (540) 552-4641.

Ramsey's Draft Wilderness

Ramsey's Draft contains one of the largest remaining stands of old-growth forest in the northern tier of the Southern Appalachians.

An original forest covering nearly 1,800 acres lies in the northern part of the wilderness, at the headwaters of Ramsey's Draft itself. Draft is the local name for a stream.

There, stream-side trees like Eastern hemlocks and cove hardwoods such as sugar maple, beech and basswood dominate the landscape. Many of the hemlocks are 300 years old and older. The hemlock woolly adelgid, a pest that kills hemlocks, has begun to infest

Hiker pauses under hemlocks in Ramsey's Draft Wilderness.

these venerable trees.

The federal government has owned the Ramsey's Draft area since 1913. The Forest Service has managed the old-growth remnant as a protected area since 1935, when it was designated as one of the first research natural areas in the country.

Ramsey's Draft, part of the George Washington National Forest, attained wilderness designation in 1984. Congress set aside 6,518 acres.

Ramsey's Draft helps mark a Civil War historical spot. Just outside the southern end of the wilderness boundary is Mountain House picnic area, named after a tollhouse along the old Staunton-Parkersburg Turnpike.

Nearby, Confederates built fortifications called breastworks to defend Shenandoah Mountain from the west.

In the 1930s, Civilian Conservation Corps crews built several trails in the area and improved a road that crossed Ramsey's Draft in 16 places. In 1969, rains from Hurricane Camille washed out most of the fords, closing the road. A 1985 flood relocated the stream channel, leaving logs and debris piled up along the stream. In 1996, Hurricane Fran caused additional channel relocations and debris jams.

Ramsey's Draft contains seven trails. The lower part of the Ramsey's Draft Trail is unmarked and interrupted by several washouts requiring challenging stream crossings during high water. Hardscrabble Knob, at 4,282 feet, is the highest point in the wilderness.

In spring, parts of Ramsey's Draft turn into a snow-white sea of mountain laurel flowers. A 1984 study documented 255 species of vascular plants in the wilderness, an unusually rich diversity.

Ramsey's Draft is about 30 miles northwest of Staunton in northwestern Virginia.

RAMSEY'S DRAFT WILDERNESS
Size: 6,518 acres.
Year designated: 1984.

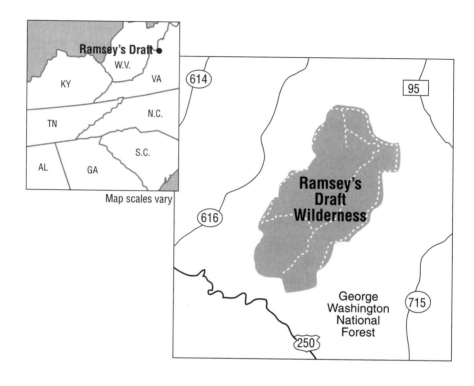

Public land unit: George Washington National Forest.
Features: 1,794-acre stand of old-growth forest.
Representative wildlife: Black bear; pileated woodpecker; brook trout.
Wilderness map: The 1:24,000-scale Ramsey's Draft Wilderness map.
U.S.G.S. topographic maps: Palo Alto; West Augusta.
Counties: Augusta; Highland.
Information: Deerfield Ranger District, George Washington National Forest, Route 6, Box 419, Staunton, VA 24401. (540) 885-8028.

Rich Hole Wilderness
Rough Mountain Wilderness

Remoteness, pockets of old-growth trees and an abundance of wildlife give these two wildernesses in the George Washington National Forest special appeal.

Each longer than it is wide, the two wildernesses run along two mountains. Rich Hole follows Brushy Mountain and Rough Moun-

186

tain, fittingly, goes along Rough Mountain. The wildernesses are about two miles apart.

A mixture of rock outcroppings and old-growth hardwoods highlight Rich Hole. About 10 to 15 percent of Rich Hole's 6,450 acres contains old-growth hemlocks along stream sides. Some of the trees are six feet in diameter and may be more than 200 years old.

On the top of 3,266-foot-high Brushy Mountain, with its double crest, are hollows up to 500 feet deep that drain into the main creeks. It is from the rich soils in these "holes" that Rich Hole gets its name.

The wilderness includes the upper watersheds of the North Fork of Simpson Creek and Alum Creek.

Rich Hole's lone maintained trail of 6.5 miles is in the southern part of the wilderness, following North Branch.

Rough Mountain may appeal more to hunters than to hikers.

A dry upland hardwood forest mixed with pitch and Table Mountain pine spreads across Rough Mountain's slopes, from 1,150 to 2,842 feet.

The 9,300-acre wilderness, designated in 1988, remains a kind of island because access to its only trail is not contiguous to national forest lands.

The Crane Trail is bounded on the east side by a railroad and the west side by private lands. No rights-of-way immediately exist, meaning people who get to the trail are trespassing unless they obtain permission from landowners.

The Forest Service has identified Forest Road 462 as the legal access to the wilderness. It is on the north side of Rough Mountain, off State Road 42, and leads to the boundary.

Rough Mountain's wildlife includes black bear, white-tailed deer and wild turkey.

It has a number of rare plants, including Kate's mountain clover, western wallflower, mountain pimpernel, northern bedstraw, white hairy leather flower, Millboro leather flower and the federally endangered shale-barren rockcress.

Both wildernesses lie from 20 to 30 miles west of Lexington, just west of Interstate 64.

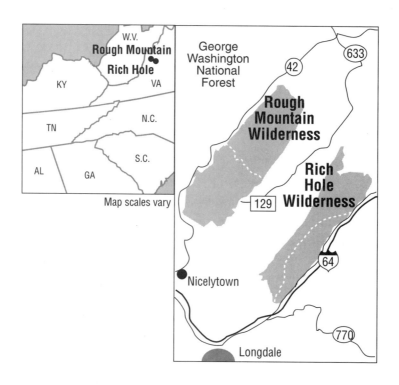

RICH HOLE WILDERNESS
Size: 6,450 acres.
Year designated: 1988.
Public land unit: George Washington National Forest.
Features: Old-growth hemlocks, rock outcroppings.
Representative wildlife: White-tailed deer, wild turkey, grouse.
Wilderness map: Black-and-white brochure.
U.S.G.S. topographic maps: Collierstown; Longdale Furnace; Millboro; Nimrod Hall.
Counties: Alleghany; Rockbridge.
Information: James River Ranger District, 810A Madison Ave., Covington, VA 24426. (540) 962-2214.

ROUGH MOUNTAIN WILDERNESS
Size: 9,300 acres.
Year designated: 1988.
Public land unit: George Washington National Forest.
Features: Pine-hardwood forest.

188

Representative wildlife: White-tailed deer, black bear, wild turkey.
Wilderness map: Black-and-white brochure.
U.S.G.S. topographic maps: Longdale Funnel; Nimrod Hall.
Counties: Alleghany; Bath.
Information: Warm Springs Ranger District, George Washington National Forest, Route 2, Box 30, Hot Springs, VA 24445. (540) 839-2521.

Saint Mary's Wilderness

Nature is reclaiming Saint Mary's, once heavily mined for minerals.

Mining began in the early 1900s. Miners worked iron ore and manganese ore mines until the 1950s, leaving piles of tailings scattered about the area.

Use of the railroad and vehicle roads continued in Saint Mary's until they were closed in the 1960s. That's when the area became part of George Washington National Forest.

Nearly 10,000 acres was designated as Saint Mary's Wilderness in 1984. Today, the remains of Saint Mary's mining legacy such as

Cool waters of Saint Mary's River in Saint Mary's Wilderness invite swimmers.

189

cement footings and spoil piles can still be seen along the wilderness's main trail.

That trail follows the river for two miles, terminating at entrances on the west and east sides of the wilderness. The trail narrows occasionally, the result of wash-outs from past floods of the Saint Mary's River.

The Saint Mary's River begins within the wilderness near Flint Mountain. At Saint Mary's Falls, the river forms pools and cascades in a small canyon formed by steep cliffs.

Above the river, quartzite cliffs crumble into talus slopes, rock slides that become pulverized into gravel.

Elevations in Saint Mary's range from 1,700 feet at the point the river leaves the wilderness to 3,640 feet on Cellar Mountain. The Blue Ridge Parkway runs along the southern edge, providing access to trails descending into Saint Mary's.

Wildlife thrives in Saint Mary's, once part of a 32,000-acre game

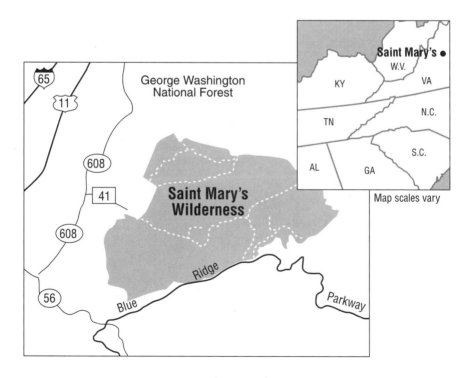

refuge.

Camping is prohibited for 300 feet around the Saint Mary's parking lot, and within 500 feet of Saint Mary's Falls. Campfires are prohibited within 150 feet of the Saint Mary's trail between and including the parking lot and the Saint Mary's Falls area.

The 1993 revision of the George Washington National Forest Land Management Plan recommended expanding Saint Mary's by 1,453 acres along its southwestern boundary.

Saint Mary's is about midway between Waynesboro and Buena Vista, between Interstate 81 and the Blue Ridge Parkway.

SAINT MARY'S WILDERNESS
Size: 9,835 acres.
Year designated: 1984.
Public land unit: George Washington National Forest.
Features: Quartzite slopes; small gorge.
Representative wildlife: Black bear; white-tailed deer; brook trout.
Wilderness maps: The 1:24,000-scale Saint Mary's Wilderness map; black-and -white brochure.
U.S.G.S. topographic maps: Big Levels; Vesuvius.
County: Augusta.
Information: Pedlar Ranger District, George Washington National Forest, 2424 Magnolia Ave., Buena Vista, VA 24416. (540) 261-6105.

Shawvers Run Wilderness

See Barbours Creek Wilderness for a description of Shawvers Run Wilderness.

Shenandoah National Park Wilderness

Forests have reclaimed nearly all of Shenandoah National Park, where farms and homesteads stood in the 1920s.

Wilderness areas lie throughout the 80-mile-long park that follows the crest of the Blue Ridge Mountains in northern Virginia.

The wilderness areas, set aside by Congress in 1978, make up 79,579 acres of ridges and valleys. Though scattered, the areas form the largest wilderness in the Southern Appalachians.

Shenandoah was authorized in 1925 when Congress approved creation of a park in the Appalachian mountains. Shenandoah's sponsors favored a park of 521,000 acres, originally the park's authorized size.

In 1936, after Virginia gave 176,500 acres to the federal government, Shenandoah entered the national park system. With additional land donations, the park grew to its present size of 196,000 acres.

Whether Shenandoah ever can expand through private land donations and exchanges came into doubt in 1995. Members of Congress from Virginia proposed limiting Shenandoah's authorized size to 196,000 acres. Such a limit would conflict with a park service study that says the park should take in areas important to maintaining the park's integrity.

The Skyline Drive runs through the elongated park. Most of the park's 500 miles of hiking trails criss cross the drive. The Appalachian Trail parallels the drive, meandering for 101 miles through the park.

White-tailed deer nibbles on grass in Shenandoah National Park.

Shenandoah illustrates how nature can reestablish a maturing forest in five decades or so. A renewed forest means a renewal of wildlife. With older-growth trees that provide forage and den sites, black bears once again prosper in Shenandoah.

The park has about 250 to 300 bears, about 200 fewer than Great Smoky Mountains National Park, which is more than twice as large as Shenandoah.

Other creatures thrive in Shenandoah's forests and

Cascading waterfall in Whiteoak Canyon abuts wilderness area in Shenandoah National Park.

meadows. Wild turkey, white-tailed deer, bobcats and skunks make a living among the chestnut oaks, white oaks, red maples, white pines and Eastern hemlocks.

The park's forests at altitudes between 3,000 and 4,000 feet attract some "Canadian" species of birds, including the Canada warbler, the black-throated blue warbler and the solitary vireo.

Little old-growth forest remains because of forest clearing that goes back to the 1700s. The largest stand consists of massive hemlocks at Limberlost at milepost 42.6. Limberlost adjoins wilderness areas that border the Whiteoak Canyon. In the southern part of Shenandoah, the wilderness section below the Big Run Overlook is undergoing renewal after a 1986 fire burned more than 4,400 acres.

While the fire benefits the wilderness, other disturbances wreak harm on Shenandoah's ecosystems.

• Ozone air pollution blankets the park, damaging plants and trees. Airborne pollutants, primarily sulfate aerosols, scatter light and re-

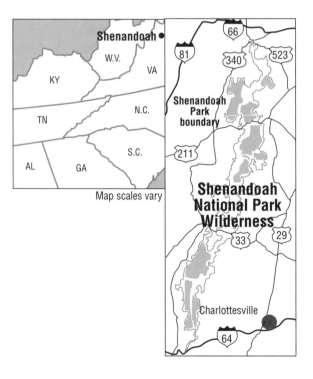

duce visibility.

• Acid rain, snow and cloud water cause lethal and sub-lethal effects on fish and other aquatic life.

• The gypsy moth, an accidental import from Europe, has devastated thousands of acres by stripping trees of their leaves.

SHENANDOAH WILDERNESS
Size: 79,579 acres.
Year designated: 1978.
Public land unit: Shenandoah National Park.
Features: Maturing forest; waterfalls; panoramic vistas.
Representative wildlife: Black bear; white-tailed deer, brook trout.
Wilderness maps: The Potomac Appalachian Trail Club publishes maps showing the park's wilderness areas. Write the club at 118 Park Street SE, Vienna, VA 22180.
U.S.G.S. topographic maps: Bentonville; Chester Gap; Flint Hill; Front Royal; Luray; Massies Corner; Old Rag; Rileyville; Strasburg; Thornton Gap; Washington; Woodville. **Counties:** Albemarle; Augusta; Greene; Madison; Nelson; Page; Rappahannock; Rockingham; Warren.
Information: Shenandoah National Park, 3655 U.S. Highway 211E, Luray, VA 22835. (540) 999-3500.

Thunder Ridge Wilderness

See James River Face Wilderness for a description of Thunder Ridge Wilderness.

Sir, what a wonderful difference thirty years makes in the country! Why, at the time I was caught by the Indians, you would not have walked out in any direction for more than a mile without shooting a buck or a bear. There were then thousands of buffaloes on the hills in Kentucky; the land looked as if would never become poor; and the hunt in those days was pleasure indeed. But when I was left to myself on the banks of the Green River, I daresay for the last time in my life, a few signs only of deer were to be seen, and, as to a deer itself, I saw none.

— Frontiersman Daniel Boone in a conversation with John James Audubon in *The Ornithological Biography*, Edinburgh, 1831-1839.

197

WEST VIRGINIA

Cranberry Wilderness

Cranberry represents a renaissance of wilderness, one that began more than 80 years ago.

The second-largest national forest wilderness in the Southern Appalachians, Cranberry spreads over 35,864 acres of mixed hardwoods and red spruce in southeastern West Virginia.

Loggers cut over Cranberry from 1915 through 1925, taking out some of the last stands of virgin timber in the Allegheny Mountains.

In 1936, a huge fire swept over much of the stump-studded area, scorching the landscape and creating an appearance of stark desolation.

But time and nature have restored Cranberry. Today, a lush, second-growth forest covers this section of the Monongahela National Forest. The wilderness provides a black bear sanctuary and habitat for animals ranging from bobcats to the federally endangered Virginia northern flying squirrel. The clear, cold streams support wild populations of native brook trout.

The mountains that make up Cranberry are broad and massive, cleaved by deep, narrow valleys. Elevation in the wilderness climbs from 2,400 to 4,600 feet. In winter, snowfalls average 80 inches a year.

Red spruce dominates the upper elevations, giving way to yel-

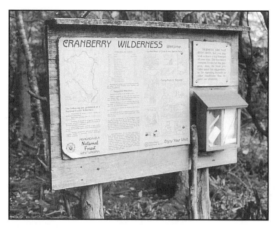

Sign marks boundary to Cranberry Wilderness.

low birch and hemlocks, then hardwoods at the lower elevations. In autumn, the mixture of beech, birches, maples and cherry flame with color against the dark green of the conifers. Among its rare species are balsam fir and Canada anemone, according to the West Virginia Natural Heritage Program.

The forest canopy shelters the entire drainage area of the Middle Fork of the Williams River and, partly, the main Williams River and the South Fork of the Cranberry River.

Deposits of coal lie under Cranberry. When Congress created the wilderness in 1983, it bought the rights to privately owned coal deposits. Congress also authorized payments up to $2.2 million to Pocahontas and Webster counties to compensate them from loss of tax revenues they could have received if the coal had been mined.

Cranberry draws its name from natural cranberry bogs just outside the southern edge of the wilderness. The bogs are the largest group of bogs in West Virginia. They belong to the "muskeg" ecosystem more commonly found farther north in New England and Canada.

Known as the Cranberry Glades botanical area, the bogs contain plants associated with acidic wetlands, including snake-mouth orchids, sundews and skunk cabbage. A half-mile-long boardwalk goes through two of the bogs.

The Monongahela National Forest maintains 12 trails totalling 72 miles in Cranberry. Many of them connect with and lead into trails in the adjoining Cranberry Backcountry, which adjoins Cranberry on the west. The 7,890-acre Cranberry Backcountry forms an area of nearly 44,000 roadless acres with Cranberry Wilderness.

The eastern edge of Cranberry Wilderness is bounded by a paved scenic drive called the Highland Scenic Highway. The 43-mile highway starts at Richwood, runs east as State Road 39-55 to State Road 150, then turns north on State Road 150 at the Cranberry Mountain Visitor Center. From there it runs along the eastern boundary of Cranberry. Along the Highland Scenic Highway are turnoffs at trailheads that lead westward into the wilderness. The highway eventually intersects U.S. 219 north of Marlinton.

The Williams River and Forest Road 86 form the northern boundary of the wilderness while the South Fork of Cranberry River and Forest Road 102 form the southern edge.

Cranberry Wilderness has 11 marked trails covering 72 miles. In winter, cross-country skiers and snowshoers follow designated trails for travel in the snow. The Forest Service warns that visitors should take caution in crossing streams during high water and should be prepared for extreme weather changes year round.

Cranberry is the most heavily visited wilderness in West Virginia. To maintain wilderness solitude, the Forest Service limits the maxi-

Cranberry Wilderness looms over tufts of cotton grass in adjoining Cranberry Glades Botanical Area.

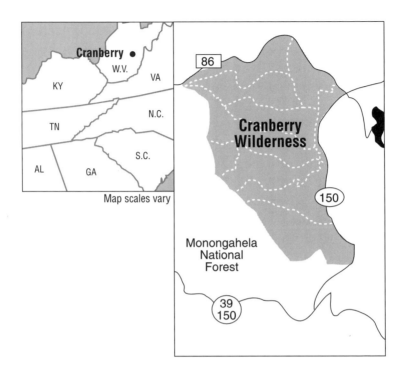

mum size for a single group to 10 people.

Cranberry is about 50 miles east of Summersville at U.S. 19 and about 50 miles north of I-64 near White Sulfur Springs.

CRANBERRY WILDERNESS
Size: 35,864 acres.
Year designated: 1983.
Public land unit: Monongahela National Forest.
Features: Broad mountains and deep, narrow valleys; mixed hardwoods with red spruce stands.
Representative wildlife: Black bear, snowshoe hare, brook trout.
Wilderness map: None.
U.S.G.S. topographic maps: Hillsboro; Lobelia; Webster Springs Southeast, Webster Springs Southwest, Woodrow
Counties: Pocahantas; Webster.
Information: Gauley Ranger District, Box 110, Richwood, WVA 26261. (304) 846-2695.

202

Dolly Sods Wilderness

A high-elevation forest of red spruce and muskeg-type bogs convey a Maine North Woods feel to this Southern Appalachians outpost.

A 10,215-acre wilderness, Dolly Sods was hewn from some of the highest parts of the Monongahela National Forest in 1975. It is the northernmost of any Southern Appalachian wilderness.

Once, Dolly Sods held some of the largest trees in the East. Red spruce trees averaging four feet in diameter stood in a layer of peat humus seven to nine feet deep. Some hemlocks measured seven feet in diameter. The virgin forest disappeared in the late 1800s when loggers moved through, taking out the original trees.

In the loggers' wake, wildfires burned the debris of limbs and roots, destroying the fertile humus layer. Charred roots and stumps still can be seen in the upper elevations. During the past 100 years, a second-growth forest emerged from the devastation. But the spruce, lacking the nutrients provided by a thick layer of humus, have only reached a diameter of 12 inches or so.

Common lore holds that the name of Dolly Sod was derived from a German pioneer family named Dahle. The Dahle family grazed

Red Creek pours over ledge in Dolly Sods Wilderness.

their livestock in open grassy areas called "sods," or meadows. These grassy areas and heath barrens were formed after the logging of the 1800s. Later, farmers moved in to create pasture for their livestock.

The wilderness begins on a 4,000-foot-high, wind-swept plateau. The rocky plateau cradles upland bogs. The wet, spongy soil hosts cranberries, blueberries and sphagnum moss. The rolling terrain offers vistas of the surrounding plateau and surrounding mountains.

Much of the plateau has no trees. What trees are there are stunted yellow birches and "one-sided" red spruces, half their foliage sheared off by shards of ice driven by strong winds.

To the west, the plateau falls off into a deep gorge. An aromatic spruce forest mixed with hardwoods like beech and maples dominates. The forest cover protects the lower Red Creek watershed. Red Creek and its tributary streams cut through the center of Dolly Sods, cascading 1.400 feet. The river descends through steep gorges and creates sluices and waterfalls that splash over rosy-colored rocks. Crossing can be very dangerous in high water.

One of the most spectacular settings in the wilderness is a waterfall on Red Creek. No bridges span the creek. Hikers should be careful when fording the creek in high water. During springtime runoffs, the water rises quickly.

Ferns, rhododendron and mountain laurel give the wilderness a thick, dark-green understory. The moist soil nourishes wildflowers such as thistle, ox-eye daisies, buttercup, hawkweed, wild bleeding heart and violets. Rare species include northern blue violet, roundleaf sundew and white monkshood.

Beaver make ponds in the bogs, the descendants of beaver that were stocked in the Monongahela National Forest beginning in 1934. Black bear and white-tailed deer roam the hardwood coves and upland spruce forest.

The wilderness gets an average of 120 to 150 inches of snow a year. During winter, it becomes inaccessible to all but the most hardy. The Forest Services closes Forest Road 75, which forms the eastern boundary of the wilderness, because of freeze-thaw damage to the thin soils.

The military used Dolly Sods for training exercises in World War II and some live mortars remain. If you find a shell, don't touch it. Note the location and report the shell to the District Ranger in Petersburg.

Because of the popularity of Dolly Sods, which could lead to over-use, the Forest Service recommends that visitors consider exploring the adjacent Flatrock/Roaring Plains Backcountry area just south of the wilderness. Flatrock/Roaring Plains is 1,000 feet higher than much of Dolly Sods.

Dolly Sods has 13 trails extending 40.4 miles in the wilderness. It lies a few miles southeast of the only national wildlife refuge in the Southern Appalachians, the Canaan Valley National Wildlife Refuge. The refuge, created in 1994, potentially will embrace more than 20,000 acres of Canadian-like wetlands and uplands.

Dolly Sods is in eastern West Virginia about 10 miles east of Canaan Valley State Park and about 50 miles east of Elkins.

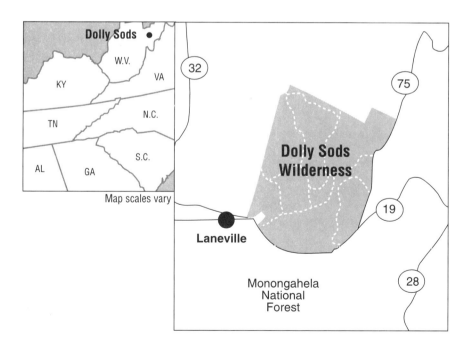

DOLLY SODS WILDERNESS
Size: 10,215 acres.
Year designated: 1975.
Public land unit: Monongahela National Forest.
Features: Red spruce forest, high-altitude bogs, deep gorge.
Representative wildlife: Black bear, beaver, hawks.
Wilderness map: None.
U.S.G.S. topographic maps: Blackbird Knob; Blackwater Falls; Laneville; Hopeville.
Counties: Grant; Tucker.
Information: Potomac Ranger District, HC 59, Box 240, Petersburg, WV 26847-9502. (304) 257-4488.

Laurel Fork North and South Wildernesses

Wedged in a valley between two mountains, the two Laurel Fork wildernesses embrace a rushing stream of the same name and the headwaters of its watershed.

The two wildernesses are separated only by a road and a campground.

Laurel Fork South (5,997 acres) covers the upper part of Laurel Fork and the watershed. Laurel Fork North (6,055 acres), a few hundred yards away, the lower part.

Remnant sign guides hikers in Laurel Fork South Wilderness.

Rich Mountain on the east and Middle Mountain on the west cup this small wilderness in the Monongahela National Forest in northeastern West Virginia. Elevation ranges from 2,900 to 3,700 feet.

The Laurel Fork Lumber Co. owned the area in the early 1900s and logged the original forest. After logging ended in 1921, wildfires swept the area. Old railroad ties for the logging trains can still be seen on some trails.

The Forest Service purchased the Laurel Fork drainage in the 1920s. Some timber cutting occurred between 1921 and

206

1963. The Civilian Conservation Corps built a camp in the 1930s at the site of the present campground. Civilian Conservation Corps workers built roads and fought forest fires in the area that is now wilderness.

The original forest consisted of red spruce, hemlocks and mixed hardwoods. The logging eliminated most of the spruce and hemlocks, changing the makeup of the forest to that of mixed hardwoods.

The dominant trees are beech, birch, black cherry and yellow poplar. Some red spruce live in the higher elevations. Scattered hemlocks remain.

Laurel Fork's wildlife includes beaver, mink, raccoon, bobcat, white-tailed deer and interior forest songbirds such as vireos and tanagers. Some black bear live here. Brown trout and brook trout swim Laurel Fork itself.

Wildflowers are abundant. Buttercup, common wood sorrel, yarrow, violets, yellow hawkweed, ramps and rue anemone are com-

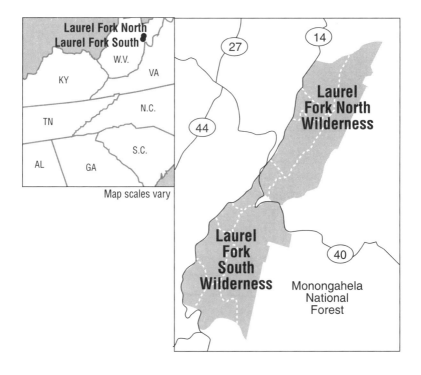

mon. Rare species include glade spurge and ostrich fern.

Laurel Fork's main trail passes through wide meadows and terminates at the campground between the two wildernesses.

The Laurel Fork Wildernesses are about 30 miles southeast of Elkins and about five miles west of Spruce Knob, at 4,861 feet the highest point in West Virginia.

LAUREL FORK NORTH AND SOUTH WILDERNESSES
Size: 12,052 acres.
Year designated: 1983.
Public land unit: Monongahela National Forest.
Features: A long forested creek valley, with grassy openings, surrounded by steep narrow ridges.
Representative wildlife: Black bear, bobcat, mink.
Wilderness map: None.
U.S.G.S. topographic maps: The Sinks of Gandy; Glady.
County: Randolph.
Information: Greenbrier Ranger District, Box 67, Bartow, WV 24920. (304) 456-3335.

Mountain Lake Wilderness

See Virginia section for the description of the Mountain Lake Wilderness.

Otter Creek Wilderness

Otter Creek blends a maturing forest with an abundance of wildlife in northeastern West Virginia.

The wilderness encompasses 20,000 acres, offering a network of 44 miles of trails through the mountainous terrain and fast-flowing streams.

The wilderness protects almost the entire drainage of Otter Creek and Shavers Lick Run. Otter Creek itself flows through the heart of the wilderness as it drops 1,200 feet from its starting height of 3,050 feet.

Loggers moved into the Otter Creek area in the early 1890s, establishing railroads and logging camps from 1905 to 1915. Timber debris left on the scarred mountains provided fuel for forest fires, which burned over most of the area.

A few years later, the federal government began buying the charred landscape. In 1920 Otter Creek became part of the newly created Monongahela National Forest.

Further timber cutting occurred in parts of Otter Creek between 1958 and 1972. Logging ceased in 1975 when Congress designated 20,000 acres as wilderness.

Some patches of old-growth forest remain. A 55-acre stand of hemlock, red spruce and yellow birch prosper within the 190-acre "Shavers Mountain Virgin Conifer" Natural Landmark. It is along the Shavers Mountain Trail (No. 129).

Now covered with a maturing, 70-year-old forest, Otter Creek has begun to mimic its original state. Black bear have returned. So have white-tailed deer, turkey, grouse and snowshoe hare.

One endangered animal, the Virginia northern flying squirrel, is

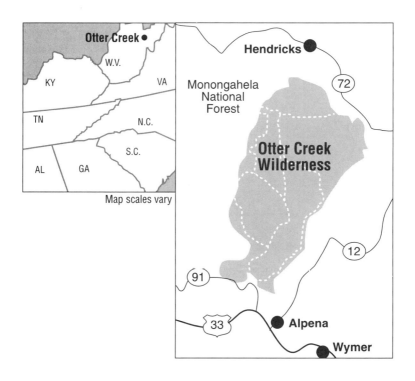

known to live here. The federally-endangered running buffalo clover is also found here as is the Cheat Mountain salamander, a threatened species.

Hikers and hunters make use of the 44 miles of trails. A few cross-country skiers come in winter.

Otter Creek is about 15 miles east of Elkins and about 20 miles west of Canaan Valley State Park.

OTTER CREEK WILDERNESS
Size: 20,000 acres.
Year designated: 1975.
Public land unit: Monongahela National Forest.
Features: Maturing hardwood-conifer forest; virgin forest remnants.
Representative wildlife: Black bear, grouse, brook trout.
Wilderness map: None.
U.S.G.S. topographic maps: Parsons; Mozark Mountain; Bowden, Harman.
Counties: Randolph; Tucker.
Information: Cheat Ranger District, Box 368, Parsons, WV 26287. (304) 478-3251.

Full moon rises over Great Smoky Mountains National Park Proposed Wilderness in NC and TN.

Other wilderness assessments

Seven federal Southern Appalachian land units with wild lands have no designated or proposed wilderness areas. Here's a brief look at wilderness assessments, if any, for each.

• Big South Fork National River and Recreation Area, Kentucky and Tennessee. Created in 1974, the Recreation Area covers 118,000 acres surrounding the Big South Fork of the Cumberland River as it flows through a rugged gorge in Kentucky and Tennessee.

Conservationists in the 1980s proposed designating 19,000 acres as the "Troublesome-Difficulty Wilderness." Neither the Forest Service, which managed the land in the 1980s, nor the National Park Service, which took over in 1990, has recommended any wilderness. The law creating Big South Fork sets aside some 56,000 roadless acres along the gorge as a virtual wilderness.

• Blue Ridge Parkway, Waynesboro, Va. to Cherokee, N.C. The National Park Service owns 78,675 acres in this national park that runs from Waynesboro, Virginia, to Cherokee, North Carolina. The Wilderness Society in 1989 suggested two possible tracts for wilderness, Rock Castle Gorge near milestone 170 in Virginia and Basin Cove near milepost 240 in North Carolina. Parkway officials said a 1990 review found the lands too small to qualify for wilderness.

• Canaan Valley National Wildlife Refuge, West Virginia. The refuge was established in 1994 a few miles northwest of Dolly Sods Wilderness. The refuge acquisition boundary encloses more than

20,000 acres of wetlands and uplands within the 3,200-foot-high valley. As of 1997, the refuge had acquired 750 acres. No wilderness study is planned.

• Little River Canyon National Preserve, Alabama. The National Park Service preserve was created in 1992 in northeast Alabama from 8,580 acres acquired from Alabama Power Co. The preserve eventually will contain more than 13,000 acres along the 800-foot-deep Little River canyon. No wilderness study has been done.

• New River Gorge National River, Gauley River National Recreation Area and Bluestone National Scenic River, West Virginia. National Park Service managers say wilderness studies were not required for the three units.

Potential wilderness areas

Future wilderness areas in the Southern Appalachians will be drawn almost entirely from national forest lands.

Some 808,000 acres of roadless areas on the 11 national forests in the region will form the core for potential wilderness consideration.

Roadless areas are national forest lands determined by the Forest Service to qualify as possible wilderness. By law, the Forest Service is to study roadless areas for a possible recommendation for wilderness designation by Congress. Under the Wilderness Act, the Forest Service's definition of a roadless area is a naturally appearing tract that has no more than a half mile of improved road for every 1,000 acres and provides outstanding opportunities for solitude and backcountry recreation.

Citizens get a chance to urge that areas studied for wilderness be recommended by the Forest Service during revisions of long-term forest management plans. The National Forest Management Act of 1976 requires each national forest to revise its plans every 10 to 15 years. The timetable is different for each forest.

Here are some prospective wilderness sites favored by pro-wilderness groups such as The Wilderness Society and the Sierra Club. Many sites take in wild lands now zoned by the Forest Service for general use such as timber cutting as well as roadless areas. Consequently, the acreages for sites listed exceed roadless area

215

acreages.

Alabama

The Bankhead National Forest has no roadless areas. The Talladega National Forest has five roadless areas consisting of 19,874 acres. Among the sites favored by conservationists are:

• Blue Mountain (Talladega), 4,797 acres. Now managed as a semiprimitive area, Blue Mountain's forest is composed primarily of second-growth oak, hickory and pine trees on ridges and slopes. Clay and Cleburne counties.

• Cheaha Additions A & B (Talladega), 945 acres. Cheaha Addition A consists of 230 acres of former state park land lying on the northern boundary of Cheaha Wilderness. Cheaha Addition B consists of 715 acres on the southeastern boundary. Clay County.

• Dugger Mountain (Talladega), 15,000 acres. Dugger Mountain holds one of the last large blocks of unbroken forest in Alabama. An upland oak-hickory forest studded with rock outcrops occurs on the mountain top and upper slopes. The Alabama Environmental Council initiated legislation for the proposed wilderness in 1996. Calhoun and Cleburne counties.

• Oakey Mountain (Talladega), 6,080 acres. Oakey Mountain is a high ridge covered with a variety of forest types. The Pinhoti Trail runs through this area. Calhoun and Cleburne counties.

Georgia

The Chattahoochee National Forest has 20 roadless areas consisting of 61,557 acres. Among the sites favored by conservationists are:

• Blood Mountain Extensions, 2,000 acres. The additions consist of three areas. The largest would protect the strip of forest between Blood Mountain Wilderness and DeSoto Falls Scenic Area. Lumpkin County.

• Brasstown Extensions, 2,000 acres. Both additions are made up of steep slopes on the southern side of Brasstown Wilderness. Towns and Union counties.

• Buzzard Knob, 8,500 acres. The Appalachian Trail crosses the crest of 3,697-foot-high Buzzard Knob. More than 400 acres of old-growth oak and hickory trees grow on the crest and western slopes. Rabun and Towns counties.

• Cohutta Extensions, 4,500 acres. These two extensions on either side of Cohutta Wilderness would protect streams that flow into Jacks River. Fannin and Murray counties.

• Ellicott Rock Extension, 1,000 acres. This extension would add critical watershed lands to the western side of Ellicott Rock Wilderness. Rabun County.

• Kelly Ridge-Moccasin Creek, 13,500 acres. Waterfalls, a primitive trout stream and pockets of old-growth oaks and hickories mark this area on the north side of Tray Mountain Wilderness. Rabun and Towns counties.

• Mountaintown, 12,000 acres. Rich in wildflowers, Mountaintown contains pockets of old-growth forest and waterfalls. It adjoins Cohutta Wilderness on the southeast side. Fannin and Gilmer counties.

• Mark Trail Extensions, 4,500 acres. Two of the extensions would fill out the narrow waist of Mark Trail Wilderness and would protect interior forest species. Towns, Union and White counties.

• Patterson Gap, 5,500 acres. The diverse landscape includes north-facing coves, steep slopes, rock outcroppings and Appalachian bogs. Rabun County.

• Rabun Bald, 14,000 acres. Georgia conservationists have fought to stave off logging in this botanically rich area. Half the area is roadless. It surrounds Rabun Bald, at 4,696 feet the second-highest peak in Georgia. Rabun County.

• Raven Cliffs Extensions, 8,000 acres. Three additions would nearly double the size of Raven Cliffs Wilderness. Most of the area already is designated for backcountry recreation and riparian protection. Lumpkin and Union counties.

• Rich Mountain Extension, 5,500 acres. Anchored by 4,075-foot-high Big Bald, the extension would fit along the northern boundary of Rich Mountain Wilderness. Fannin and Gilmer counties.

• Rock Gorge, 4,500 acres. A relatively wild, undisturbed area, Rock Gorge would link 6,500 acres across the Chattooga River in South Carolina to form a new wilderness. The area borders Ellicott Rock Wilderness. Rabun County.

• Rocky Face, 6,600 acres. Located just west of Interstate 75, Rocky Face holds old-growth stands and prime stream habitat for trout and Coosa bass. Walker and Whitfield counties.

• Southern Nantahala Extensions, 6,500 acres. These four remote tracts provides prime habitat for black bear and cliff-nesting birds on the southern tier of Southern Nantahala Wilderness. Rabun and Towns counties.

• Tray Mountain Extension, 1,500 acres. Perched on the northwestern side of Tray Mountain Wilderness, this is an area of steep slopes and stream headwaters. Towns County.

Kentucky

The Daniel Boone National Forest has one roadless area consisting of 1,890 acres.

Among the sites favored by conservationists are:

• Beaver Creek Expansion, about 12,000 acres. Expansion of the Beaver Creek Wilderness would take in ridges surrounding the wilderness as well as adjacent upland oak-pine forest. The area includes potential habitat for the red-cockaded woodpecker, an endangered species. McCreary County.

• Cave Creek wild area, part of the Beaver Creek Expansion. Adjacent to the northwestern boundary of the Beaver Creek Wilderness, the land is underlain by an undisturbed system of caverns. McCreary and Pulaski counties.

• Jellico Mountain, 40,000 acres. This largely roadless area along the Tennessee line contains prime examples of mixed hardwood forests. McCreary and Whitley counties.

• Wolfpen Creek, 1,890 acres. Bounded by Clifty Wilderness on the east, Wolfpen Creek has sandstone cliffs and a heavily used segment of the Sheltowee Trace National Recreation Trail. Menifee

County.

North Carolina

The Nantahala National Forest has 12 roadless areas consisting of 40,773 acres. The Pisgah National Forest has 16 roadless areas consisting of 83,628 acres. The acreages include those for the five Wilderness Study Areas.

Among the sites favored by conservationists are:

• Bald Mountains (Pisgah), 13,000 acres. Old trees, rock outcrops and native trout streams make this an outstanding wild area. This area, combined with 12,000 adjoining acres in Tennessee, forms the Bald Mountain complex. Madison County.

• Black Mountains (Pisgah), 14,000 acres. Forming the eastern flank of Mount Mitchell, at 6,684 feet the highest peak in the East, the area has been a top priority for wilderness by conservationists. Yancey County.

• Cheoah Bald (Nantahala), 13,000 acres. Though reduced in size from road building and logging in the 1980s, conservationists consider this area a top candidate for wilderness. Ten miles of the Appalachian Trail pass through Cheoah Bald. Graham and Swain counties.

• Joyce Kilmer-Slickrock Extensions (Nantahala), 9,000 acres. Flanking the eastern and southern sides of Joyce Kilmer-Slickrock Wilderness, the areas would safeguard views and help form a corridor to Great Smoky Mountains National Park. Graham County.

• Linville Gorge Extensions (Pisgah), 3,000 acres. Two areas zoned for timber cutting would buttress the eastern and southern sides of Linville Gorge Wilderness. Burke County.

• Middle Prong and Shining Rock Extensions (Pisgah), 6,000 acres. These areas would augment Middle Prong Wilderness and extend Shining Rock Wilderness to the Blue Ridge Parkway. Haywood County.

• Southern Nantahala Extensions (Nantahala), 17,000 acres. Six areas provide logical extensions of Southern Nantahala Wilderness to protect backcountry trails and black bear habitat. Clay and Macon counties.

• South Mills River (Pisgah), 17,000 acres. One of the largest remaining wild lands in the Pisgah forest, this area adjoins the southeast border of the Cradle of Forestry. Henderson and Transylvania counties.

• Tusquitee Bald (Nantahala), 27,000 acres. Black bear habitat and trout streams highlight this remote wild area named for 5,200-foot-high Tusquitee Bald. Cherokee, Clay and Macon counties.

South Carolina

The Sumter National Forest has four roadless areas consisting of 6,161 acres. Among the sites favored by conservationists are:

• Chauga, 16,000 acres. The area contains part of the Chauga River, being studied for National Wild and Scenic River designation, and much of its surrounding watershed. Rare animals include the Southern Appalachian woodrat and New England cottontail. Oconee County.

• Ellicott Rock Extension, 2,000 acres. These watershed lands of the Chattooga River adjoin Ellicott Rock Wilderness on the east and south. The Forest Service recommended the area for wilderness in 1985. Oconee County.

• Persimmon Mountain, 7,000 acres. A transition zone between the mountains and the Piedmont, Persimmon Mountain offers a mix of plants that includes mountain camellia and enchanter's nightshade. Oconee County.

• Rock Gorge, 6,500 acres. Named for a canyon on the Chattooga River, Rock Gorge would join 3,500 acres in Georgia for a new wilderness. The area borders Ellicott Rock Wilderness. Oconee County.

Tennessee

The Cherokee National Forest has 18 roadless areas consisting of 86,805 acres. Among the sites favored by conservationists are:

• Bald Mountain, 12,017 acres. Part of a roadless complex of

25,000 acres, Bald Mountain contains abundant black bear. The area joins 13,000 acres of wild lands in North Carolina. Greene County.

• Bald River Gorge Extension, 1,737 acres. Lying on the west side of Bald River Gorge Wilderness, this area would add interior habitat and protect headwaters. Monroe County.

• Big Laurel Branch Extension, 6,240 acres. Four miles of the Appalachian Trail traverse this wild land along the spine of Iron Mountain on the north side of Big Laurel Branch Wilderness. Carter and Johnson counties.

• Big Frog Extensions, 7,300 acres. Flanking the side of Big Frog Wilderness, these two areas would add a missing tract from the northern wilderness boundary to perimeter roads and power lines. Polk County.

• Flint Mill, 13,765 acres. Part of Holston Mountain, Flint Mill includes a 7-mile segment of the Appalachian Trail. Carter, Johnson and Sullivan counties.

• Gee Creek Extension, 4,200 acres. Wrapping around Gee Creek Wilderness on three sides, the extension would enlarge the Cherokee forest's smallest wilderness by 1,700 acres. McMinn and Polk counties.

• Joyce Kilmer-Slickrock Extension, 5,198 acres. The area follows the northern boundary of Joyce Kilmer-Slickrock Wilderness. Monroe County.

• Little Frog Mountain Extensions, 3,500 acres. These two areas would help safeguard the visual quality of the forest from the Ocoee River across U.S. 64 from Little Frog Mountain Wilderness. Polk County.

• Rogers Ridge, 5,255 acres. Just south of the Mount Rogers National Recreation Area, Rogers Ridge contains high grassy ridges that offer spectacular views of surrounding mountains. Johnson County.

• Sampson Mountain Extension, 6,308 acres. This area, along the eastern boundary of Sampson Mountain Wilderness, contains rare plants such as piratebush, John's cabbage and marsh marigold. Unicoi and Washington counties.

• Slide Hollow, 4,353 acres. Lying east of White Rocks Mountain, Slide Hollow contains old-growth hardwood stands and unfragmented forest habitat. Carter County.

• Unaka Mountain Extensions, 5,900 acres. One extension includes the 910-acre Unaka Mountain Scenic Area on the west border of the Unaka Mountain Wilderness. The other takes in the Rattlesnake Ridge and Dark Hollow areas on the northern side. Unicoi County.

• Upper Bald River, 14,333 acres. Some of the wildest land in the national forest, the area would border the Bald River Gorge Wilderness on the east and south. Monroe County.

Virginia

The George Washington National Forest has 27 roadless areas consisting of 245,432 acres. The Jefferson National Forest has 39 roadless areas consisting of 163,894 acres. Among the sites favored by conservationists are:

• Barbours Creek Addition (Jefferson), 806 acres. This addition would extend the northeastern corner of Barbours Creek Wilderness. Botetourt and Craig counties.

• Bear Creek (Jefferson), 18,253 acres. This is the largest roadless area on the Jefferson forest. The area contains several of Virginia's few remaining pure stands of Table Mountain Pine and a section of the Appalachian Trail. Smith and Wythe counties.

• Beartown Addition (Jefferson), 4,459 acres. Surrounding the southern side of Beartown Wilderness, the addition takes in part of the Appalachian Trail and the Chestnut Knob shelter on the trail. Bland and Tazewell counties.

• Big Schloss (George Washington), 20,755 acres. Big Schloss is known for its sandstone outcrops and white rock cliffs. The Big Blue Trail traverses the area. Fredrick and Shenandoah counties, Va., and Hardy County, W.Va.

• Broad Run (Jefferson), 10,994 acres. This is a relatively remote and steep roadless area. Botetourt and Craig counties.

• Crawford Mountain (George Washington), 9,868 acres. This

area in the Allegheny Mountain range is considered one of the three best black bear habitats in Virginia outside Shenandoah National Park. Augusta County.

• Hoop Hole (Jefferson), 5,444 acres. Hikers using 10 miles of the National Recreation Trail cross Stony Run, a stream with several waterfalls in a gorge filled with mountain laurel. Botetourt County.

• Hunting Creek-Little Wolf Creek (Jefferson), 8,961 acres. Beaver ponds and marshes in a gorge-like valley form the centerpiece of the Little Wolf Creek area, crossed by the Appalachian Trail. Bland County.

• James River Face Addition (Jefferson), 1,261 acres. Tucked into the southeastern corner of James River Face Wilderness, the addition includes the Piney Ridge Trail. Amherst County.

• Kimberling Creek Additions (Jefferson), 281 acres. Popular with hunters, these two additions to the Kimberling Creek Wilderness includes Sulphur Spring Fork, a stream that flows over a solid rock bottom. Bland County.

• Little Dry Run Addition (Jefferson), 3,000 acres. This addition would more than double the size of Little Dry Run Wilderness. Grayson, Smith and Wythe counties.

• Little River (George Washington), 27,248 acres. This is the largest national forest roadless area in the Southern Appalachians. The high ridges and knobs offer spectacular vistas of Shenandoah Valley. Augusta and Rockingham counties.

• Little Wilson Creek Additions (Jefferson), 1,729 acres. The larger of the two additions to Little Wilson Creek Wilderness takes in a northern hardwood forest of birch, beech and maple. Grayson County.

• Mountain Lake Additions (Jefferson), 6,492 acres. Three additions to the Mountain Lake Wilderness includes the Kire Mountain area, which connects to the West Virginia portion of the wilderness. Craig and Giles counties, Va., Monroe County, W.Va.

• Peters Mountain Additions (Jefferson), 4,523 acres. Two additions bracket Peters Mountain Wilderness, encompassing the Appalachian Trail and the Allegheny Trail. Giles County.

• Ramsey's Draft Addition (George Washington), 12,771 acres. The area surrounds Ramsey's Draft Wilderness on all sides and would triple the size of the existing wilderness area. Augusta and Highland counties.

• Saint Mary's Addition (George Washington), 1,453 acres. The Forest Service recommended in 1993 enlarging Saint Mary's Wilderness but no legislation has been introduced. The area lies along the southern boundary.

• Shawvers Run Additions (Jefferson), 2,858 acres. Two areas, on the northwest and southwest sides of Shawvers Run Wilderness, include Hanging Rock, a 240-acre geologic area with panoramic views. Craig County.

• Southern Massanutten (George Washington), 11,919 acres. The roadless area, five miles west of Shenandoah National Park, contains an 80-year-old forest of chestnut oak, white oak, Table Mountain and pitch pine. Page and Rockingham counties.

• The Priest (George Washington), 5,742 acres. The Forest Service in 1993 recommended wilderness designation but no legislation has been introduced. Named after a 4,063-foot-high mountain, this area is located along the forest's eastern boundary in central Virginia and includes a stretch of the Appalachian Trail. Nelson County.

• Three Ridges (George Washington), 4,748 acres. The Forest Service in 1993 recommended wilderness designation but no legislation has been introduced. Three Ridges lies north of The Priest, across the Tye River.

• Wilson Mountain (Jefferson), 5,100 acres. Just east of the James River, Wilson Mountain takes in a segment of the Sprouts Run National Recreation Trail. Botetourt and Rockbridge counties.

West Virginia

The Monongahela National Forest has 17 semi-primitive, non-motorized areas consisting of 130,669 acres, roughly equivalent to roadless areas. The George Washington National Forest has two roadless acres consisting of 28,068 acres.

Among the sites favored by conservationists are:

• Big Schloss (George Washington), 20,755 acres. The largest roadless area in the forest, Big Schloss is known for its sandstone outcrops and white rock cliffs. The Big Blue Trail traverses the area. Hardy County, W.Va., and Fredrick and Shenandoah counties, Va.

• Dolly Sods North (Monongahela), 6,169 acres. Lying adjacent to the northern border of Dolly Sods Wilderness, this area was acquired in 1993. It contains sedge meadows, heath plains, bogs and stunted spruce forests. The endangered Cheat Mountain salamander lives here. Grant and Tucker counties.

Waterfall tumbles over cliff in Sipsey Wilderness in Alabama.

Appendix

Here are the headquarters for U.S. Forest Service and National Park Service wilderness areas, proposed wilderness areas and wilderness study areas.

Alabama

WILLIAM B. BANKHEAD NATIONAL FOREST
Size: 180,581 acres.
Year created: 1918.
Location: Northwest Alabama.
Wilderness: 25,002 acres.
Percent of land in wilderness: 14 percent.
Address: National Forests in Alabama, 2946 Chestnut St., Montgomery, AL 36107.
Phone: (334) 832-4470.

TALLADEGA NATIONAL FOREST
Size: 387,220 acres.
Year created: 1936.
Location: East-central, west-central Alabama.
Wilderness: 7,297 acres.
Percent of land in wilderness: 2 percent.
Address: National Forests in Alabama, 2946 Chestnut St., Montgomery, AL 36107.
Phone: (334) 832-4470.

Georgia

CHATTAHOOCHEE NATIONAL FOREST
Size: 749,512 acres.
Year created: 1936.
Location: North Georgia.
Wilderness: 114,789 acres.
Percent of land in wilderness: 15 percent.
Address: Chattahoochee-Oconee National Forest, 508 Oak St. NW, Gainesville, GA 30501.
Phone: (770) 536-0541.

Kentucky

CUMBERLAND GAP NATIONAL HISTORICAL PARK
Size: 20,274 acres.
Year created: 1955.
Location: Southeast Kentucky; northeast Tennessee, west Virginia.
Wilderness: None (6,375 acres proposed, with another 3,810 acres of potential wilderness).
Percent of land in wilderness: 0 percent
Address: Cumberland Gap National Historical Park, Box 1848, Middlesboro, KY 40965.
Phone: (606) 248-2817.

DANIEL BOONE NATIONAL FOREST
Size: 690,987 acres.
Year created: 1936.
Location: Southern, central Kentucky.
Wilderness: 17,437 acres.
Percent of land in wilderness: 3 percent.
Address: Daniel Boone National Forest, 1700 Bypass Road, Winchester, KY 40391.
Phone: (606) 745-3100.

North Carolina

GREAT SMOKY MOUNTAINS NATIONAL PARK
Size: 520,409 acres.
Year created: 1934.
Location: Western North Carolina; eastern Tennessee.
Wilderness: None (up to 466,000 acres proposed).
Percent of land in wilderness: 0 percent.
Address: Great Smoky Mountains National Park, 107 Park Headquarters Road, Gatlinburg, TN 37738.
Phone: (423) 436-1200.

NANTAHALA NATIONAL FOREST
Size: 528,223 acres.
Year created: 1920.
Location: Western North Carolina.
Wilderness: 28,900 acres (wilderness study areas cover an additional 11,690 acres).
Percent of land in wilderness: 6 percent.

Address: National Forests in North Carolina, Box 2750, Asheville, NC 28802.
Phone: (704) 257-4200.

PISGAH NATIONAL FOREST
Size: 504,790 acres.
Year created: 1916.
Location: Western North Carolina.
Wilderness: 37,945 acres (wilderness study areas cover an additional 15,230 acres).
Percent of land in wilderness: 8 percent.
Address: National Forests in North Carolina, Box 2750, Asheville, NC 28802.
Phone: (704) 257-4200.

South Carolina

SUMTER NATIONAL FOREST
Size: 359,567 acres.
Year created: 1936.
Location: Northwest, central South Carolina.
Wilderness: 2,859 acres.
Percent of land in wilderness: 1 percent.
Address: Francis Marion-Sumter National Forest, 4931 Broad River Road, Columbia, SC 29210-4021.
Phone: (803) 561-4000.

Tennessee

CHEROKEE NATIONAL FOREST
Size: 633,156 acres.
Year created: 1920.
Location: Eastern Tennessee.
Wilderness: 66,389 acres.
Percent of land in wilderness: 10 percent.
Address: Cherokee National Forest, P.O. Box 2010, Cleveland, TN 37320. Phone: (423) 476-9700.

GREAT SMOKY MOUNTAINS NATIONAL PARK
Size: 520,409 acres.
Year created: 1934.

Location: Western North Carolina; eastern Tennessee.
Wilderness: None (up to 466,000 acres proposed).
Percent of land in wilderness: 0 percent.
Address: Great Smoky Mountains National Park, 107 Park Headquarters Road, Gatlinburg, TN 37738.
Phone: (423) 436-1200.

Virginia

GEORGE WASHINGTON NATIONAL FOREST
Size: 1,064,562 acres.
Year created: 1918.
Location: Northern, central Virginia; eastern West Virginia.
Wilderness: 32,209 acres.
Percent of land in wilderness: 3 percent.
Address: George Washington and Jefferson National Forests, 5162 Valleypointe Parkway, Roanoke, VA 24019-3050.
Phone: (540) 265-5100.

JEFFERSON NATIONAL FOREST
Size: 716,073 acres.
Year created: 1936.
Location: Western, southwest Virginia; southeast Kentucky; southern West Virginia.
Wilderness: 57,655 acres.
Percent of land in wilderness: 5 percent.
Address: George Washington and Jefferson National Forests, 5162 Valleypointe Parkway, Roanoke, VA 24019-3050.
Phone: (540) 265-5100.

SHENANDOAH NATIONAL PARK
Size: 196,000 acres.
Year created: 1936.
Location: Northern Virginia.
Wilderness: 79,579 acres.
Percent of land wilderness: 41 percent.
Address: Shenandoah National Park, 3655 U.S. Hwy. 211E, Luray, VA 22835.
Phone: (540) 999-3500.

West Virginia

MONONGAHELA NATIONAL FOREST
Size: 909,084 acres.
Year created: 1920.
Location: Eastern West Virginia.
Wilderness: 77,951 acres.
Percent of land in wilderness: 9 percent.
Address: Monongahela National Forest, 200 Sycamore Street, Elkins, WVA 26241.
Phone: (304) 636-1800.

National Forest wilderness sign signifies land is part of National Wilderness Preservation System.

Trail books

Here are hiking guidebooks that cover wilderness areas, proposed wildernesses and wilderness study areas in the eight Southern Appalachian states. This list is not intended to be complete.

Alabama
Alabama Trails, by Patricia Stenger Sharpe, The University of Alabama Press, Tuscaloosa, Ala. 1993.

Georgia
The Georgia Conservancy's Guide to the North Georgia Mountains, edited by Fred Brown and Nell Jones, The Georgia Conservancy, Atlanta, Ga. 1990.

The Hiking Trails of North Georgia, by Tim Homan. Peachtree Publishers, Ltd., Atlanta, Ga. 1997.

The Hiker's Guide to Georgia, by Donald W. Pfitzer, Falcon Press Publishing Co., Helena, Mont. 1993.

Kentucky
The Historic Cumberland Plateau/An Explorer's Guide, by Russ Manning, University of Tennessee Press, Knoxville, Tenn. 1993.

Kentucky's Land of the Arches, by Robert H. Ruchhoft, The Pucelle Press, Cincinnati, Ohio. 1986.

Hiking Kentucky/Scenic Trails of the Bluegrass State, by Darcy and Robert Folzenlogen, Willow Press, Littleton, Colo. 1995.

North Carolina
Day and Overnight Hikes in the Great Smoky Mountains National Park, by Johnny Molloy, Menasha Ridge Press, Birmingham, Ala. 1995.

Hiking Trails of Joyce Kilmer-Slickrock and Citico Creek Wilderness Areas, by Tim Homan, Peachtree Publishers, Ltd., Atlanta, Ga. 1990.

Hiking Trails of the Smokies, Great Smoky Mountains Natural History Association, Gatlinburg, Tenn. 1994.

Hiking Great Smoky Mountains, by Rodney and Priscilla Albright, The Globe Pequot

Press, Old Saybrook, Conn. 1994.

Hiking North Carolina, by Randy Johnson, Falcon Press Publishing Co. Inc., Helena, Mont. 1996

North Carolina Hiking Trails, by Allen de Hart, Appalachian Mountain Club Books, Boston, Mass. 1996.

The Best of the Great Smoky Mountains National Park/A Hiker's Guide to Trails and Attractions, by Russ Manning and Sondra Jamieson, Mountain Laurel Place, Norris, Tenn. 1991.

South Carolina
Hiking South Carolina Trails, by Allen de Hart, The Globe Pequot Press, Old Saybrook, Conn. 1994

Tennessee
Day and Overnight Hikes in the Great Smoky Mountains National Park, by Johnny Molloy, Menasha Ridge Press, Birmingham, Ala. 1995.

Hiking Great Smoky Mountains, by Rodney and Priscilla Albright, The Globe Pequot Press, Old Saybrook, Conn. 1994.

Hiking Tennessee, by Kelley Roark, Falcon Press Publishing Co. Inc., Helena, Mont. 1996.

Hiking Tennessee Trails, by Evan Means, The Globe Pequot Press, Old Saybrook, Conn. 1994.

Hiking Trails of Joyce Kilmer-Slickrock and Citico Creek Wilderness Areas, by Tim Homan, Peachtree Publishers, Ltd., Atlanta, Ga. 1990.

Hiking Trails of the Smokies, Great Smoky Mountains Natural Association, Gatlinburg, Tenn. 1994.

Tennessee Trails, by Evan Means, The Globe Pequot Press, Old Saybrook, Conn. 1994.

The Best of the Great Smoky Mountains National Park/A Hiker's Guide to Trails and Attractions, by Russ Manning and Sondra Jamieson, Mountain Laurel Place, Norris, Tenn. 1991.

Wilderness Trails of Tennessee's Cherokee National Forest, edited by William H. Skelton, University of Tennessee Press, Knoxville, Tenn. 1992.

Virginia
Circuit Hikes in Shenandoah National Park, by James W. Denton, Potomac Appalachian Trail Club, Vienna, Va. 1990.

Hiking Virginia's National Forests, by Karin Wuertz-Schaefer, The Globe Pequot Press, Old Saybrook, Conn. 1994.

The Hiker's Guide to Virginia, by Randy Johnson, Falcon Press Publishing Co., Helena, Mont. 1992.

The Trails of Virginia/Hiking the Old Dominion, by Allen de Hart, The University of North Carolina Press, Chapel Hill, N.C. 1995.

Wilderness Virginia/A Guide to Hiking Virginia's National Forest Wilderness Areas, by Steven Carroll and Mark Miller, Old Forge Productions, Lexington, Va. 1995.

West Virginia
Hiking the Mountain State/The Trails of West Virginia, by Allen de Hart, Appalachian Mountain Club Books, Boston, Mass. 1986.

Monongahela National Forest Hiking Guide, by Bruce Sundquist and Allen de Hart, Fifth Edition, West Virginia Highlands Conservancy, Charleston, W.Va. 1988.

United States
America's Wilderness/The Complete Guide to More Than 600 National Wilderness Areas, by Buck Tilton, Foghorn Press, San Francisco, Calif. 1996.

The Big Outside/A Descriptive Inventory of the Big Wilderness Areas of the United States, by Dave Foreman and Howie Wolke, Harmony Books, New York, NY. 1992.

Bibliography

A Survey of West Virginia Mammals. Charleston: The West Virginia Conservation Commission, 1951.

America's Wilderness/Twenty-Five Years of Wilderness Preservation 1964-1989. Washington, D.C.: The Wilderness Society, 1989.

Aplet, Gregory H., and Boone, D. Daniel. *Sustaining Biodiversity in the Southern Appalachians.* Washington: The Wilderness Society, 1994.

America's Wilderness. Washington: The Wilderness Society, 1989.

Belue, Ted Franklin. *The Buffalo East of the Mississippi River.* Murray, Ky., 1991.

Brickell, John. *The Natural History of North-Carolina*, New York: Johnson Reprint Corp., 1969.

Brooks, Maurice. *The Appalachians.* Boston: Houghton Mifflin Co., 1965.

Buxton, Barry M. and Crutchfield, Malinda L. *The Great Forest: An Appalachian Story.* Boone, N.C.: The Appalachian Consortium Press, 1985.

Byrd, William. *A Journey to the Land of Eden and Other Papers*, edited by Mark Van Doren. New York: Macy-Masius, The Vanguard Press, 1928.

Catesby, Mark. *Catesby's Birds of Colonial America*, edited by Alan Feduccia. Chapel Hill: University of North Carolina Press, 1985.

Davis, Mary Byrd. *Old Growth in the East/A Survey.* Richmond, Vt.: Wild Earth, 1993.

Davis, Mary Byrd. *Eastern Old-Growth Forests/Prospects for Rediscovery and Recovery.* Island Press, Washington, D.C. 1996.

Earley, Lawrence S. *Return of the Natives.* Raleigh: Wildlife in North Carolina, 1991.

Fifty Year History of the Monongahela National Forest. Elkins: Monongahela National Forest, 1970.

Final Supplement to the Final Environmental Impact Statement, Volume I, Nantahala and Pisgah National Forests, North Carolina. Asheville: U.S. Forest Service, 1994.

Frome, Michael. *Battle for the Wilderness.* New York: Praeger Publishers, 1974.

Goldman, Edward A., and Young, Stanley P. *The Puma.* New York: Dover Publications, Inc., 1946.

Harper, Francis. *The Travels of William Bartram.* New Haven: Yale University Press, 1958.

Healy, Robert G., and Shands, William E. *The Lands Nobody Wanted.* Washington: The Conservation Foundation, 1977.

Houk, Rose. *Great Smoky Mountains National Park/A Natural History Guide.* New York: Houghton Mifflin Co., 1993.

Irwin, Hugh. *Biological Diversity in the Southern Appalachian Highlands: Southern Appalachian Highland Ecoregion Task Force.* The Sierra Club: 1994.

Irwin, Hugh. *Tennessee's Mountain Treasures/The Unprotected Wildlands of the Cherokee National Forest.* Atlanta: The Wilderness Society, 1996.

Jackson, Laura E. *Mountain Treasures at Risk.* Atlanta: The Wilderness Society, 1989.

Johnson, Randy. *Southern Snow/The Winter Guide to Dixie.* Boston: Appalachian Mountain Club, 1987.

Jones, Perry. *The European Wild Boar in North Carolina.* Raleigh: North Carolina Wildlife Resources Commission, 1972.

Keen, Richard A. *Skywatch East/A Weather Guide.* Golden: Fulcrum Publishing, 1992.

Kercheval, Samuel. *A History of the Valley of Virginia.* Strasburg: Shenandoah Publishing House, 1925.

Kricher, John C., and Morrison, Gordon. *A Field Guide to Eastern Forests.* Boston: Houghton Mifflin Company, 1988.

Lambert, Darwin. *The Undying Past of Shenandoah National Park.* Boulder: Roberts Rinehart, Inc. Publishers, in cooperation with Shenandoah Natural History Association, 1989.

Lambert, Robert S. *Logging in the Great Smoky Mountains National Park/A Report to the Superintendent.* Gatlinburg: Great Smoky Mountains National Park, 1958.

Land and Research Management Plan, Chattahoochee-Oconee National Forests. Gainesville, Ga., 1987.

Land and Research Management Plan, Cherokee National Forest. Cleveland, Tenn., 1986.

Land and Research Management Plan, Daniel Boone National Forest. Winchester, Ky., 1987.

Land and Research Management Plan, Revised, George Washington National Forest. Harrisonburg, Va., 1993.

Land and Research Management Plan, Jefferson National Forest. Roanoke, Va., 1985.

Land and Research Management Plan, Monongahela National Forest. Elkins, W.Va., 1986.

Land and Research Management Plan, National Forests in Alabama. Montgomery, Ala., 1986.

Land and Research Management Plan, Sumter National Forest. Columbia, S.C., 1985.

Lawson, John. *A New Voyage to Carolina*, edited by Hugh Talmage Lefler. Chapel Hill: The University of North Carolina Press, 1967.

Lederer, John. *The Discoveries of John Lederer.* Charlottesville: The University of Virginia Press, 1958.

Logan, John H. *A History of the Upper Country of South Carolina from the Earliest Periods to the Close of the War of Independence.* Charleston: S.G. Courtenay and Company; Columbia, P.B. Glass,

1859.

Long, James R. (Bob). *Biodiversity and Reintroduction of Extirpated Species.* Knoxville: The University of Tennessee, 1994.

Long, James R. (Bob). *Feasibility Assessment for the Reintroduction of North America Elk into Great Smoky Mountains National Park.* Knoxville: The University of Tennessee, 1996.

Lowerre, Nan, and Mastran, Shelley Smith. *Mountaineers and Rangers: A History of Federal Forest Management in the Southern Appalachians 1900-81.* Washington: U.S. Department of Agriculture, 1983.

Martini, Don. *Inside the Smokies.* Sevierville: Nandel Publishing Company, 1989.

Mason, Robert L. *The Lure of the Great Smokies.* New York: Houghton Mifflin Company, 1927.

Matthiessen, Peter. *Wildlife in America.* New York: The Viking Press, 1959.

McClanahan, Rod D. *Experimental Southern Appalachians Elk Reintroduction.* Asheville: U.S. Forest Service, 1996.

McClure, Thomas J. *North Carolina's Mountain Treasures/The Unprotected Wildlands of the Nantahala and Pisgah National Forests.* Atlanta: The Wilderness Society, 1992.

McClure, Thomas J. *South Carolina's Mountain Treasures/The Unprotected Wildlands of the Andrew Pickens District of the Sumter National Forest.* Atlanta: The Wilderness Society, 1993.

McDonald, Jerry N. *North American Bison: Their Classification And Evolution.* Berkeley: University of California Press, 1981.

Morley, Margaret W. *The Carolina Mountains.* New York: Houghton Mifflin Co., 1913.

Muir, John. *A Thousand-Mile Walk to the Gulf.* Boston: Houghton Mifflin Company with Norman S. Berg, Dunwoody, Ga., 1916.

Nash, Roderick. *Wilderness and the American Mind.* New Haven: Yale University Press, 1982.

Ogburn, Charlton. *The Southern Appalachians/A Wilderness Quest.* New York: William Morrow & Co., Inc., 1975.

Parsons, Shireen. *Virginia's Mountain Treasures/The Unprotected Wildlands of the Jefferson National Forest.* Atlanta: The Wilderness Society, 1996.

Pelton, Michael R. and Long, James R. *Proposal for an Experimental Release and Habitat Evaluation for Reintroduction of Fisher into the Appalachian Ecosystem.* Knoxville: The University of Tennessee, 1993.

Savage, Henry Jr. *Lost Heritage/Wilderness America Through The Eyes Of Seven Pre-Audubon Naturalists.* New York: William Morrow & Co., Inc., 1970.

Shaffer, Mark L. *Lifelands.* Washington: The Wilderness Society, 1994.
The Southern Appalachian Assessment. Prepared by federal and state agencies, coordinated through

Southern Appalachian Man and the Biosphere Cooperative. Atlanta: U.S. Department of Agriculture, Forest Service, Southern Region, 1996.

Silverberg, Robert. *The Auk, the Dodo, and the Oryx.* New York: Thomas Y. Crowell Company, 1967.

Taylor, Mark. Seiners and Tongers: *North Carolina Fisheries in the Old and New South,* Volume LXIX, No. 1. Raleigh: The North Carolina Historical Review, 1992.

Terbourgh, John, *Where Have All the Birds Gone?* Princeton: Princeton University Press, 1989.

Terres, John K. *The Audubon Society Encyclopedia of North American Birds.* New York: Alfred A. Knopf, 1980.

The Wilderness Act Handbook. Washington, D.C.: The Wilderness Society, 1984.

Thomas, Roy Edwin. *Southern Appalachia, 1885-1915.* Jefferson, NC: McFarland & Company, 1991.

Trail of Tears National Historic Trail: Comprehensive Management and Use Plan. Washington: U.S. Department of the Interior, 1992.

Venters, Vic. *Bears in the West.* Raleigh: Wildlife in North Carolina, 1996.

Weidensaul, Scott. *Mountains of the Heart.* Golden: Fulcrum Publishing, 1994.

Williams, Samuel C. Lt. *Henry Timberlake's Memoirs, 1756-1765.* Johnson City: The Watauga Press, 1927.

Wilson, Alexander. *The American Ornithology.* Boston: 1840.

Zaslowsky, Dyan, and The Wilderness Society. *These American Lands.* New York: Henry Holt and Company, Inc., 1986.

Index

Tray Mountain Wilderness, 65, 96-98, 217, 218
Trout, brook, 42, 43, 93, 94, 120, 143, 156, 199, 207
Trout, brown, 43, 93, 120, 207
Trout, rainbow, 43, 83, 93, 120
Trout Unlimited, 125
Tusquitee Bald wild area, 220

Unaka Mountain Extensions, 222
Unaka Mountain Wilderness, 66, 162-164, 222
Unicoi Mountains, 123, 135, 158
Upper Bald River wild area, 222

Vanderbilt, George, 31
Virginia, 23, 24, 26, 31, 55, 65, 106, 107, 167-195, 222
Visibility, 56, 58

Watauga Lake, 154
Weakley, Alan, 26
Weeks Act, 31, 32
West Virginia, 23-26, 28, 30, 31, 40, 41, 43, 45, 46, 66, 199-210, 213, 214, 224
Wilderness
    history of, 35-38
Wilderness Act, 36, 215
Wilderness Society, The, 32, 35, 125, 215
Wildlife, 39
Wilson, Alexander, 26
Wilson Mountain wild area, 224
Wolf, red, 15, 43, 49, 50, 115, 118, 123
Wolf, 17, 26, 131
Wolfpen Creek wild area, 218

Yellowstone National Park, 29, 35

Zahner, Dr. Robert, 32
Zahniser, Howard, 35

This is an extension of the copyright page

A History of the Valley of Virginia, by Samuel Kercheval, © 1925, reprinted by permission of Shenandoah Publishing House Inc., Strasburg, Va.

The Appalachians, by Maurice Brooks, © 1965, reprinted by permission of Houghton Mifflin, New York.

Arnold Guyot's Notes on the Geography of the Mountain District of Western North Carolina, Myron H. Avery and Kenneth S. Boardman, eds., reprinted by permission of North Carolina Historical Review 15 (July 1938) 267, Raleigh, N.C.

Catesby's Birds of Colonial America, edited by John Feduccia, © 1985, reprinted by permission of the University of North Carolina Press, Chapel Hill, N.C.

Southern Appalachia, 1885-1915," by Roy Edwin Thomas, © 1991, reprinted by permission of McFarland & Co., Jefferson, N.C.